Leaders can't afford to stumble, stutter or say the wrong thing in front of the media. This book teaches you how to get it right by learning the crucial secrets only media insiders know. Don't talk to the media until you've read this book.

~ Judeth Wilson, Author of *The Inside Secrets of Powerful Presenters Revealed and Training Works!*

This isn't another book just filled with techniques for handling media interviews with aplomb, although it does that exceptionally well. The gift of *Media Talk* is its ability to show leaders how to communicate leadership in high-pressure, high-stakes situations. This book is a superb resource for any leader in the public eye.

~ Dr Sally J Rundle, Author of *Values Grid: Compelling Leadership Values*

This is not your typical book about what to say and what not to say to the media. It does offer solid advice and practical tools for navigating the evolving media landscape, including social media, but as importantly, it shows you how to communicate leadership in the most demanding situations. *Media Talk* is an inspiring read for any leader who's serious about using the largest audience to make the greatest impact – and difference.

~ Dr Karen Nelson-Field, *Author of Viral Marketing: The Science of Sharing*

CONTENTS

TRICIA KARP

CREATOR OF THE WISE TALK
LEADERSHIP COMMUNICATION METHOD

MEDIA
TALK

35 SECRETS YOU NEED TO KNOW
BEFORE YOU TALK TO THE MEDIA

MEDIA TALK

Cover design & typesetting: Matt Cumming, www.BookDesignHQ.com
Editor: Kris Kane
Cover photo: Victoria Berekmeri

Published by Wise Talk Press

Email: enquire@wisetalk.com.au
Website: www.wisetalk.com.au

TRICIA KARP

CREATOR OF THE WISE TALK
LEADERSHIP COMMUNICATION METHOD

MEDIA
TALK

35 SECRETS YOU NEED TO KNOW
BEFORE YOU TALK TO THE MEDIA

WISE TALK

Tricia Karp has written *the* modern media handbook. Her advice and spirit, insight and depth make this book an essential resource.

~ Nuala Hafner, Media Personality

If you're looking for a media trainer, Tricia Karp is the gold standard. Warm and wise, savvy and practical, *Media Talk* is as much a guide to navigating the complex world of media as it is a lesson in leadership communication.

~ Kate Woodland, Author of *Hiring For The Future*

Sharp, insightful and packed with practical strategies, *Media Talk* explains precisely what it takes to win the media game. A must-read book written by an expert with insider knowledge, Tricia shows you how to handle the toughest media situations and come out on top.

~ Greg Cassar, Author of *Lead Machine*

Don't talk to the media before you read this book. Full of insider secrets from someone who knows the media inside out, *Media Talk* takes the stress out of high pressure situations and puts you in the driver's seat.

~ Mark Robinson, Author of *Winning The Wealth Game*

INTRODUCTION

For over twenty years now, my profession has been performing in public, under pressure—and guiding others to do the same. I want to help people to inspire and lead, especially in high-pressure, high-stakes situations. It's become my passion.

Over the length of my career, I've worked in radio and television as a news and current affairs journalist, a commercial prime time television news presenter, a voice artist, news director, senior corporate communications adviser, entrepreneur, corporate trainer, executive coach, and workshop leader. In those roles I've watched the most seasoned CEOs pull out every trick in the book to avoid being interviewed on camera. I've worked with managing directors who took more of an interest in me than usual—by asking lots of questions to try to distract me during training sessions. I've observed leaders crumple under the pressure of a media conference and unintentionally speak words that had severe consequences. I've trained people whose nerves, anxiety, and lack of confidence undermined their authority. I've heard the stutters and shaky voices, and seen the red faces and folded arms and other body language that shouts, "I don't want to be here," and, worse, "even I don't believe what I'm saying."

As a journalist, I interviewed all types of leaders, from prime ministers to multibillionaire entrepreneurs to CEOs, from the creators of social and political movements to leaders of new and developing schools of thought, authors, activists, rock stars and Olympic athletes. Somewhere along the way I became a leader too, running my own business and being the one out in front, being interviewed by television and radio stations, newspapers and bloggers, and invited to speak at conferences and on all sorts of other stages.

I've sat on both sides of the camera and microphone, and have been frequently reminded what a tough gig it is to stare down the barrel of a TV camera and answer interview questions.

I started my journalism career at the age of twenty-one, at a commercial radio station. Back then, before the days of syndication, radio newsrooms were treated seriously and stations invested in their news services. We had half a dozen journalists more seasoned than I, and it was a vibrant and complex training ground for a young, wide-eyed reporter. Daunted by having to interview political leaders, and not really knowing what to ask, I gave plenty of free airtime to messages and stories that hadn't been appropriately prodded or poked. No wonder they always said *"Yes!"* to requests to be interviewed by me!

I didn't know it then, but it was also a fertile and compelling leadership training ground. Every day, I interviewed four or five people, and had to face the challenges of drawing my subjects out, of finding the right questions to ask. Every year, I was lucky to speak to a small handful who knew how to influence, inspire, and motivate with their words. I became fascinated by people with an ability to render a room silent when they walked in, before they even spoke, and then hold an audience in the palm of their hand. They were a rare breed, and possessed a power that not only intrigued me and made them memorable, but inspired loyalty and trust from others, often in the most trying of circumstances.

I'll never forget the impact that interviewing then Australian Prime Minister Paul Keating had upon me as a young journalist in the early 1990s. He had a charm and presence that captivated everyone in the room. With clear boundaries and a demeanour that made it plain he refused to suffer fools, he managed to speak in a way that ensured everyone listened. An imposing figure in his dark Zegna suit, he was still surprisingly warm and friendly, and exuded comfort even amid a room full of journalists. I was intrigued by Keating's powerful presence and seemingly effortless charisma. I'd marvel about the experience as I walked away with my interview on my clunky old tape recorder to take back to the newsroom, and think long and hard about what made him such a powerful, effective speaker and so at ease in such a high pressure environment.

These days, the business world is becoming increasingly complex and challenging. Navigating complexities isn't about predicting the future or reducing risk. It's about building capacity—in yourself, in your people, and in your organisation.

The business environment is volatile and uncertain. Yet people, countries, and economies are more deeply connected than ever. We live in an era where your message, speech or interview are beamed across the country, even the world, in a matter of mere seconds. The imperative to get it right is greater than ever, and the risks more devastating. Get it wrong, and you can count on your words reaching a growing and increasingly vocal and uncensored audience across various multimedia platforms. The stakes are rising; so, too, the pressure.

We're hungry for leaders we can trust. We need leaders who can inspire true followership. We crave vision and inspiration. We want wise words, well spoken. What we don't need is more information.

I believe that every time you speak, it's your job to inspire, to lead.

I believe that every time you don't lead when you speak, it's a wasted opportunity, at best, and can have dire consequences, at worst—especially in high stakes situations.

The media hold an enormous amount of power—but so do you, when you learn how to make the most of opportunities to engage with them.

In this book, I'm going to share with you the Wise Talk Leadership Communication Method. I'll show you how to confidently deal with the media without stress, especially in high-pressure situations.

I'll show you how to use your presence to stand out, and do it in a way that is natural and authentic to you, and engaging and captivating for your audiences.

This isn't about performing or showmanship. It's not about being excessively confident, no matter the situation. Those days are long gone.

This is about being more of yourself, and building greater trust and followership along the way.

This is about making a difference for you, your company and your community.

CHAPTER 1:

IT STARTS WITH PRESENCE

Presence is something we all recognise—when you see it, you know it. Someone walks in the room and heads turn. When that person speaks, people listen. When they lead, others follow.

Confidence and comfort are the domain of people with strong presence. They think and speak clearly and persuasively, even under pressure. They act with purpose and intention. They take responsibility for themselves and their results. They're authentic. They own what they say and do, and it matches who they are.

How you're perceived dictates decisions and actions. Job applicants oozing with confidence and showing excellent people skills often win over candidates who are more technically qualified. Buyers make purchases based on the presence and persuasiveness of a salesperson. Managers with a powerful presence persuade the best people to come and work with them. They can increase and turn around performance, enhancing the work of individuals and teams under their guidance. Communities, organisations, states, and countries often elect their leaders based on the power of their presence, usually conveyed via the media.

A strong presence can benefit anyone, regardless of your role. A strong presence creates powerful business outcomes. It's an *X* factor, potentially a game changer... and it's crucial in high-stakes communications.

Most people struggle to articulate how to get it, and how to further cultivate that perception of presence is even more of a mystery. Some people think you're born with it—or you're not. The truth is, anyone can develop a more powerful presence.

When I lead workshop programs, I ask people to think of someone they know who has a powerful presence. I ask what it is about that particular person that makes him or her stand out. These are the sorts of answers I usually get:

- He walks his talk
- She's confident and comfortable in herself
- He performs well under pressure
- When she walks into a room, people notice her and listen to what she says
- He dresses impeccably well
- She leaves a lasting impression when she speaks
- He inspires action
- She easily conveys a clear message

Then I ask participants what it is that these people do—or don't do—that projects a strong presence? Typically, I'm met with silence.

A lack of presence is a serious barrier for any leader. Common perceptions I hear include:

- He's too stiff
- She looks nervous when she speaks
- She's too tentative
- She knows her stuff, but gets off track and forgets what she's saying

- He needs more confidence
- He's too intense and makes people feel uncomfortable
- She has trouble running a meeting when there are lots of strong personalities in the room
- He doesn't use the appropriate language
- He's too laid back
- She's technically brilliant, but not well-liked
- Not enough people buy into his vision
- He can't make a difference when trying to deal with performance issues
- She doesn't take a stand on the important issues

None of that is a recipe for trust.

I want to give you a framework that enables anyone to expand her or his leadership presence by taking practical action steps. It's an integrated approach that incorporates your assumptions and beliefs, communication skills, and your physical energy. It sits at the heart of taking the stress out of high-pressure, high-stakes communications.

Acting techniques are popular among proponents of developing presence by emphasising a physical, or "outside-in" approach. It's just a small part of the story though, and too much focus on the physical creates a leadership presence that isn't genuine. True presence requires alignment, addresses the whole person, and creates sustainable change and results.

Think about the leader, for example, who has spent time preparing for her radio interview. She has a clear message, is well-organised, has a powerful vision, and has worked very hard to ensure she speaks with authority. What she hasn't done is question her assumptions about doing a live on-air interview, especially with a talkback host who's renowned for being tough. Those assumptions have made her feel nervous, unsure and inferior. No matter how hard she tries, the words she speaks don't match what people are experiencing from her voice. Her assumptions of not being good enough can be heard in her shakiness and hesitation to answer certain questions, and her presence fades with every sentence she speaks.

Consider also the spokesman who's undertaken many media interviews, nailed his key messages, and put on his suit jacket and straightened his tie to look the part before the TV crew arrives. What he hasn't done is considered that his job is to speak to—and put first—his audience rather than the journalist, during the interview. His thoughts that the questions being asked are too simple and superficial are written all over his face. He also hasn't considered that, after an incident with a particularly aggressive reporter a few years ago, he carries much disdain for the media in general. He frowns, sighs, and gazes at the journalist condescendingly. Regardless of knowing what he's talking about and being considered a leader in his industry, he appears to his viewing audience as arrogant, undermining, and untrustworthy.

We process everything through our language, whether it's verbally or physically. Our thoughts show up in our body language and actions. Others can read us. It has a major impact on our presence.

Researchers have discovered that humans can make and process ten thousand facial expressions, mostly unconsciously. What's even more amazing is we have the ability to interpret these facial expressions when we see them on others.

In high-pressure situations, that can be detrimental.

The Wise Talk Leadership Communication method has three principles—and associated behaviours—to help you create a strong presence. It sits at the heart of speaking wisely and well, and suffering less stress, especially in high- stakes communication situations. The principles are:

- Purposeful
- Personal
- Powerful

I often refer to them as the 3Ps, or P3. Choose whichever works best for you to remember the formula.

Here's how each of the steps helps you to create a stronger presence. This is an essential part of your preparation before we get to the skills and techniques for competently dealing with the media.

PURPOSEFUL

Purposeful communication is about understanding how you want to be perceived, and then communicating in a way to ensure that perception. It means aligning your thoughts with your words and actions.

That sounds simple, but it takes finely tuned self-awareness and an understanding of the impact you have on others. It means determining the conversations going on in your head, and how they might need to change. They never stop, by the way, and are rolling around in there even when you're not paying attention.

I hear negative thoughts and beliefs from my clients all the time, including, from those who are open enough to admit it:

- I don't have anything to say that's important
- I'm worried the media will take me out of context
- I'm not interesting enough
- I'm an introvert, so I can't comfortably draw attention to myself
- I'm worried that I'll say the wrong thing and get my company in trouble
- I don't have what it takes
- I'm not good in these situations
- I'll freeze up and forget what I'm saying
- The media are out to get me
- Journalists just want news that's negative and will make what I say seem worse than it is
- I look terrible on camera
- I don't sound like a leader should and no one takes me seriously

For those who aren't so verbal with their thoughts, their secret misgivings and doubts are clearly evident from their body language and actions alone. From the CEO who suddenly became a skilled interviewer and asked all sorts of questions to try to distract me from filming him present and offering feedback, to the manager who suddenly had something "urgent" arise which meant he could only spend fifteen minutes with me for a media coaching session—rather than the two hours we'd had set aside (that was after he'd already twice rescheduled the session). And then there was the young leader who was renowned in her organisation for her technical brilliance and her confidence in meetings, who bared her true thoughts in a media training session by swallowing her words throughout the on-camera interviews all while turning a bright shade of red.

If you're investing in thoughts and ideas that are negative, it'll be showing up in your presence. Neuroscientists have discovered that our intentions shape how our brain functions. And guess what? Those intentions create shortcuts in our minds that become the path of least resistance. It boils down to this: the more you think something, the easier it is for your mind to process it. For example, if you're constantly telling yourself you can't stand doing media interviews and you worry you'll say the wrong thing, those thoughts will become a belief, habit and pattern. They'll show up whenever you find yourself having to do an interview.

The only way to create a different possibility is to recognise your limiting thoughts and replace them—with intention, on purpose. Then, being purposeful starts to create a new shortcut in your brain.

I've worked with many clients who, after what they described as an excruciating speaking experience, have told me they suffer anxiety and can no longer stand up in front of groups to speak at work, let alone brave a media interview. They come to me because they've subsequently arrived at the realisation that presenting is something they can no longer afford to avoid. Helen, an executive manager, admitted she felt so anxious that she was sure she'd need to run out of the room and vomit. In fact, she'd done just that on several occasions, excusing herself a few minutes before she was due to present.

In our work together, Helen realised her internal dialogue before a talk was, "You don't know what you're talking about."

We began to create a new purpose for those situations that felt right for Helen. We looked at her actions too, and where and how they weren't aligned with her purpose. She began to make a conscious effort to stop her nervous chatter before giving a talk, and not rush to the bathroom just before it was her time to speak. She also worked on creating a new shortcut in her brain.

The vomiting stopped, so too the fear, and presentations are nowhere near the big deal for her that they once were.

To have a compelling presence, you need to start by taking control of what's going on in your head. One of the best ways to do this is to consciously create your Wise Talk Brand.

It needs to be aligned with your core values and beliefs. Your Wise Talk Brand reflects your personality, but is much further reaching. It's how you aspire to communicate, and has the potential to impact all areas of your life. It's a touchstone, a statement of your aspirations to be your best.

Your behaviours, language, and actions need to match your Brand. When you notice your thoughts heading in a negative direction, you can start creating a new path of least resistance by reminding yourself of your Brand.

To discover your Wise Talk Brand, make a list of the values you want to convey. It might help to list qualities you admire in others. Then bring the list down to five, or even three values.

Come up with a statement or acronym that will be easy for you to remember. It doesn't matter what it is, as long as it's meaningful to you.

Clients have shared all sorts of Brand statements with me, including:

- Credible & Compelling
- Visionary & Vocal
- Connect, Inspire, Empower
- Inspiring & Influential
- Caring, Credible, Captivating

Once you've established your Brand, consider that different situations and circumstances often call for additional Brands. After all, how you speak in a sales pitch is different from how you answer media interview questions about a crisis—or announce good news—and different again if you're announcing a restructure and laying off staff, or presenting at an AGM.

There isn't a one-size-fits-all scenario, and you need to always be purposeful about your desired impact in each scenario.

If that sounds obvious to you, it's the rare person I've worked with who did this before we started working together. I've watched people present tough news with a strange smile on their face and squirm when given the opportunity to deliver great news. During private media coaching with one very senior person in her company, I was whacked on the leg for asking a question she stumbled to answer. None of this makes for much awareness around the desired impact.

What's important to know is that audiences don't always remember what you tell them, but they always remember how you make them feel, especially when you're delivering news that's tough to hear. Consider the mood or feeling you want to evoke in your audiences to work out the appropriate Brand for each situation, as it arises.

The best way to do this is to work out answers to these questions:

1. How do you want your audience to feel?
2. What feeling do you need to embrace and embody to ensure that happens?

I'm not talking about faking it. What I am saying is, for you to have a powerful presence, you need to be purposeful and aligned with what you're talking about—and you need to do this for all dealings with the media.

Once you've worked out the answers to those two questions,

you'll have your Brand for that particular situation. It will guide the way you speak and behave, and be an anchor if your thoughts start turning in an unhelpful direction.

PERSONAL

The next step in developing presence is about forming connections that drive loyalty and career success. It's the job of leaders to create an aura that draws others to them. They need to be knowable and approachable. They need to forge strong relationships. They need to focus on getting the best out of others by cultivating empathy and trust.

In the workplace, strong connections make for better productivity, better coworkers, and better leaders who can inspire and motivate. Connections give you influence. Many new leaders experience the frustration of learning that their title doesn't automatically command followership. Winning hearts and minds requires making yourself someone who others want to follow and trust.

Approachability creates business outcomes. Connection creates powerful results that you need to do your job well and move forward in your career.

If you consider such "soft skills" unimportant, think again. People want to work with people they like and trust. If you're someone with whom your colleagues want to work, you're going to have more opportunities for yourself, and higher levels of engagement amongst your team.

In the realm of media interviews, a leader who's guarded struggles to connect with audiences and engender trust, as does a leader who's uncomfortable and nervous—or avoids such opportunities in the first place.

It would be remiss of me not to bring up the word *vulnerability*. Before you conjure up images of group hugs and sharing circles for everyone to look into one another's eyes and share their deepest, darkest personal secrets, consider this: great presence is created by a balanced combination of power and humanity, or competency and vulnerability. That's how others connect with us.

Many of us still carry the notion that we're split in two—one version turns up to the office, while the other is saved for after hours. I've worked with some clients who even have a third version that shows up especially for media interviews and other public speaking situations.

But connection is what makes people memorable to us. Consider those who've been influential in your career, and with whom you'd jump at the chance to work with again if given the opportunity. We work harder for those with whom we feel a connection.

In my work facilitating workshop programs, there've been times when I've felt it appropriate to share my own vulnerability. It's usually a story about an experience I've had that's relevant, and it's always meant revealing some sort of struggle, and a moment of trepidation just before I do.

I've often wondered if it's the right thing to do. Every time though, the affirmation has come when my words and actions created a greater level of connection in the group, and a richer and more rewarding learning environment. My personal stories have been used to set an example, or underline important concepts that I'm teaching.

I can't tell you how often I've been thanked for sharing a part of myself. In fact, I'm commonly credited for creating a safe environment for my clients, particularly in training sessions. I have no doubt that I owe part of that to my expertise, experience, and subsequent credibility, but another big factor is my willingness and ability to balance competency with vulnerability, as appropriate.

We don't trust people who behave as though they're perfect and have all the answers. We don't trust permanent bright shiny polish. If perfectionism is your modus operandi, take heed: it will alienate you from others, and undermine you.

During a media interview, vulnerability can be extremely powerful if it means admitting a mistake, for example, or accepting that what worked in the past won't now, and it's time to revisit your vision. If you find yourself in front of a camera talking about staff members being seriously injured, and you express your distress about that, from your heart, your vulnerability will connect you with your viewers.

One of my clients, in her mid-thirties, is extremely well-accomplished, and when she talks about her work and achievements her audiences are regularly in awe. She's strong, super smart, and attractive, with an extremely powerful presence. When she walks in the room, people immediately notice her. You might call her the 'total package,' and many have.

She used to struggle to understand why she intimidated people, especially given that she works in the health field, and is dedicated to caring for others. She has since realised, in our work together, that it's important for her to drop the notion of being perfect, as the only way she truly connects with her staff—and audiences—is when she's at her most human. That means being vulnerable, as appropriate. It's changed her relationships at work, which she now describes as more connected and honest, and it's made her a much more trusted leader in whom others now regularly confide.

It is a balancing act. The key lies in navigating how to maintain power and competency while being real.

Without connection, you lack presence. You might be a polished speaker and exceed every target ever set for you, but if others can't relate to you on a human level, you won't be trusted. Admired, perhaps, but never fully trusted.

Another client, an executive manager, shared me with her frustrations with her boss who frequently sat in his office chair with his legs on his desk and his hands behind his head. He struggled to make eye contact, and my client felt as though he didn't really listen to what she said.

She described his arrogance and inability to connect with his staff and colleagues. She also described her awe and surprise when she heard him speak at a staff conference. In sharing his vision for the organisation, he relayed a personal story. He spoke about frequently working late at night, and usually getting home long after his two young sons were in bed. His children became disinterested in spending time with him on the rare occasions he was available. When he asked them why, they said, 'Because you're never here'.

He shared at the conference that that was a turning point for him in his personal and working life, and that it was important to him that everyone in the organisation left work when the office doors closed each night, and spent time at home with their families. He spoke of his vision for the organisation he wanted, which included people who had a healthy work/ life balance. He spoke from his heart and received a standing ovation from several members in the room.

My client shared with me that, during her boss's talk, she felt a connection to him in a way she hadn't before. She made an effort to thank him, and he thanked her too, saying he'd never received feedback like that before.

They connected. The boss shared his vulnerability and humanity at that conference. He showed that he wrestles with the same issues as every other parent, and he made a difference for his staff with his words and vision.

He also told a story, and stories have a profound effect on us. We remember them far more easily than facts and figures, and we use stories to make sense of one another and the world. We relay our experiences via stories every day. We share other people's stories, and we remember the stories they tell us. We compare our own experiences to the stories we hear, and we often learn valuable lessons about our own values and actions. Stories are great fodder for media interviews.

When I run workshops and present as a professional speaker, I use stories to illustrate my points. My presentations are extremely story-driven. I've seen the difference stories make so often that I wouldn't consider not including them. People's faces light up. They lean in closer to me. They smile. They nod, as if to say, "Yes, I know what that's like." Those who've been less attentive suddenly look up and take notice. Statistics, facts, and figures alone never have that power. Stories are the most direct way for people to understand what we're really about and connect with us.

Many people believe their stories aren't very interesting, and that they need to have had an amazing life experience to make them so. A friend once said to me, sarcastically, that people are only interested in hearing from those who've had a near death experience or accomplished a feat that others said was impossible. That's not true. In fact, the stories we relate to best are sourced from our every day life experiences.

I'm often asked to speak about how to tackle confronting conversations in the workplace. I open my talks with a story about working as a manager for the first time, running a radio newsroom. I had a staff member who, while she hadn't been sacked, had had life made difficult for her in her previous organisation so that she would 'choose' to move on. She ended up in my team, and I knew nothing about her history when I turned up for my first day on the job at 5.30am. In my talk, I share the way this woman greeted me at the door, calling me 'darling' and giving me a huge bear hug. I talk about my suspicions that something wasn't quite right, that were soon confirmed as I heard her make too many abusive personal phone calls and watched her do very little work. I talk about the ways she tried to endear herself to me, bringing me fresh eggs from her chooks and cakes she'd bought at roadside stalls. I talk about my complete sense of inadequacy in knowing how to deal with her, my overwhelming sense of helplessness, and the toll that took not only on me, but the rest of the team who were enthusiastic and passionate about producing first-rate news bulletins.

It's not an amazing story. But how many of us have worked with people who pushed our buttons? How many of us have worked with people whose behavior caused us stress? Lots. We relate to these stories. My story is one that's memorable and often referred to many months later when I meet people who've been in my audiences.

Storytelling has developed into a business art form. It doesn't need to be a big deal though. We all know how to tell stories. We do it every day. Stories strengthen communication and presence. They're easy to remember, and they're memorable. They also create shared meaning.

You can consider adding stories to your media interviews when you:

- Want to motivate people and paint a picture of what's possible
- Want to show people that you've been in their shoes, and you understand
- Want to encourage people to tackle something new
- Need to deliver 'bad' news and want to show empathy
- Want to demonstrate your approach, values and vision
- Are facing difficulties that relate to a situation you've experienced before
- Want to give credibility to fresh ideas by sharing past experiences
- Need to show others what you have in common

I'm often asked for a formula for telling a story. There's no right way, although stories do always include:

- A clear message, purpose or moral
- A beginning and ending, and a segue back to the topic
- Descriptions of characters and imagery and a sense of place
- Reference points the audience can understand
- A personal connection to the storyteller and/or your audience
- Conflict, vulnerability, or achievement that your audience can relate to
- Your intention strategically underlined

Whenever you tell a story, remember to watch out for perfectionism. Sharing only successes and holding back the parts that seem unimpressive or show vulnerability will sound like bragging and cut you off from your audience. It's why so many of us are fed up with hearing just the 'good news' on Facebook. It's not real.

The news is never good when it comes to rambling. Great stories are quick and to the point. Losing track of where you're up to, and going off on tangents is also something of which to be aware. Expect to lose your audience's attention when you do this, especially during a media interview. You also run the risk of 'over-sharing' and get into dangerous territory by going off-message.

Make an effort to incorporate stories into your interviews to help you master keeping it personal.

POWERFUL

I call this last P 'powerful' because you need to have the ability to communicate in a way that builds and motivates followership. It's about inspiring—rather than just informing—and moving others to action. It means you're a change agent, inspiring others to alter their thoughts, perspectives or actions. It means you're a visionary.

Visionary is a big word. It's not rocket science though. It just takes attention to develop and communicate.

Visionaries are positive. They see problems – and solutions.

When times are tough, they use their vision as a rudder to help their team stick together and get to the other side.

Visions and goals are different. Your goal might be to increase performance by 20 percent or create a product that becomes the number one bestseller in its market. Your vision might be to set a standard for innovation and risk taking, or bring happiness to your customers. Visions are always meaningful.

Visionaries take their visions very personally, and a vision doesn't go anywhere unless a leader feels it in his bones. Vision starts with leaders looking deep inside themselves to discover what's truly important.

Visionary leaders embody their vision through their presence. They provide the passion, energy and consistency to make their vision real for others, and they keep that vision alive in all interactions and communications. They use powerful language, such as, 'We're going to …'

They make bold proclamations, unlike others who fear losing credibility and would rather under promise and over deliver because it feels safer.

Visionary leaders don't start their sentences with, 'I think' or 'I might' or 'I guess' or 'I hope'. They say 'I will'. They also issue inspiring calls to action, and have no problem telling others what they need to do to fulfill their shared vision.

The importance of what I call 'spotlight opportunities' isn't lost on leaders who want to be inspirational. They make the most of being seen as a chance to share their vision and influence. They take a stand, and they're interesting and engaging when they share it. They know that staying under the radar never inspired anyone, and they use media opportunities to spread their vision.

How many interviews have you watched that were boring? How many times have you listened to a leader who you could tell was holding back?

How many times have you been the protagonist of any of the above?

Most speakers—standing up in front of a group or being interviewed—aren't amazing in the moments they need to be. Most speakers don't communicate leadership.

There are PR consultants being paid good money by organisations everywhere to come up with newsworthy angles. They're on the phone, reaching out to journalists, selling the value of their client and his story. The truth is though, all reporters really want—especially for TV and radio—is 'good talent'. If you fit the bill, they'll keep coming back for more. And more media coverage means more visibility, which means a bigger stage for a leader, her message, and her vision.

The media want charisma. They want someone who knows how to speak their language, talk in news grabs, uses memorable quotes, and is engaging, captivating, and inspiring.

As audiences, when we hear someone who dares to stand out,

he captures our attention. He's memorable, and he's invited back again and again.

Having worked with hundreds and hundreds of clients to help them become better speakers and communicate leadership, I've learnt that the wisest place to start is with authentic presence that's *purposeful, personal* and *powerful.*

CHAPTER 2:

HOW TO MASTER THE MEDIA

It's not about you. It's not about the journalist who's asking you the questions, either. Media interviews are about connecting with your audience, focusing on how to build trust, and ultimately how to inspire and lead.

If you've never heard it said like that, I'm not surprised. Traditional media trainers focus purely on what to say and what not to say. They focus on body language, from the outside in, so that there's so much more you have to think about and get right when you're facing down the spotlight and the high-pressure, rapid fire questions of a seasoned journalist.

It's not easy to have to worry about whether you're frowning and how to set your face straight when, deep down, you're anxious that you're going to say the wrong thing and you're wishing the TV reporter and cameraman would just go away—and maybe had never even contacted you in the first place.

With our ability to unconsciously read ten-thousand different facial expressions, we know when someone's spinning us a lie. All the right messaging and body language techniques in the world won't hide that. And if you're being interviewed on camera, there are no two ways about it: the camera never lies.

I want you to try an exercise. The best place for this is in front of a mirror. Think of something that makes you angry and watch your body language. Do you stare with narrowed eyes? Do you tense your shoulders? Do you keep your lips

tight? We all express anger differently, but there's no doubt the emotion is reflected in your body language.

Now, think of something that makes you happy. What happens? Does your face soften and lift? How about your eyes? What happens to your mouth, your shoulders?

We can't fake it. And it takes extraordinary effort to try.

I used to train clients in the traditional way. I've provided long lists of dot points on what they have to remember to do each time they're interviewed. I've told them to keep their answers short and succinct but never just answer with a 'yes' or 'no'. I've picked them up on words that undermine their credibility. I've told them to maintain eye contact, not rush their answers, stick with their key messages, sit up straight, stop frowning, answer questions as if they've just been asked for the first time even if they weren't, take charge of the interview, smile about the good news, start answers again if they're not happy with what they just said, be calm, cordial, confident, authoritative, respectful, not condescending …

It's a list that just made me sigh with exhaustion after I wrote it.

It's true that everything on that list is relevant, and important. But there's another way. And it's not only easier—it's far more effective and powerful, and positions you not just as the leader you are, but the leader you aspire to be.

I've never met anyone who loves being interviewed by the media. Journalists carry an enormous amount of power, and it can be intimidating. Most people faced with the task of an interview try to play it safe. They keep repeating their key messages, spend the whole time worrying they'll be asked a tough question they don't want to answer, and try to pretend that everything's just fine.

What if, regardless of how tough the questions get in an interview and how aggressive the interviewer, you could focus just on your audience?

What if you could put your attention squarely on creating a connection with your audience, and building trust, no matter how tricky or potentially damaging the topic?

What if you could take advantage of the opportunity you're being given in an interview to use the power of the media to communicate on your terms, and position yourself as a trusted leader?

I'm going to give you 35 Wise Talk Media Tips to do just that, to ensure you lead every time you speak in an interview.

This takes practice, and I guarantee you it's worth it. Mastering these skills is a game changer, not only for your credibility but also your stress levels.

Media interviews are tough. I was recently reminded of this when I was asked to appear on a national television program. Several days before the interview, the producer gave me the questions I was going to be asked. I remember thinking, 'What a lovely thing to do!' I looked through the questions and felt comfortable with them, surmising that the producer had given them to me because the interview topic wasn't in any way controversial.

As a journalist, I didn't reveal the questions I was going to ask before an interview. People rarely asked for them anyway, and for those who did I gave a general overview of the *sorts* of questions I might ask. I didn't do that to be difficult—it was important to allow for spontaneity, so that their answers would be genuine. If I planned to interview someone about a particularly contentious issue, there was no way I'd reveal my questions beforehand. Like most journalists, I did my best to fairly present both sides of the story. I also had an agenda, and a job to do, that included getting the story across the line and meeting my deadline. I'd worry that if I revealed my full hand, a potential interviewee mightn't agree to speak with me.

I'm reminded of an episode of 60 Minutes in which the 'Wolf of Wall Street', Jordan Belfort, stood up mid-interview and walked out, saying the interview was 'done'. He went on to say to his interviewer, Liz Hayes, 'I was told this was a friendly, nice interview. No-one has ever treated me as disrespectfully as you have'.

Belfort, a one-time stockbroker, did prison time for fraud and money laundering, after ripping off investors of more than 200-million dollars. His story was told in the blockbuster movie 'The Wolf of Wall Street', the rights for which he was reportedly paid nearly one million dollars.

Hayes questioned him about his current financial set-up and the amount he's repaying his victims. Prosecutors have claimed Belfort's way behind in repaying his debts, and it was both a fair and salient question. He told Hayes during the interview that she was a 'very nice woman ... but this is obviously a hatchet job', before he stormed off.

Only Belfort, his management, and the team at 60 Minutes know what the arrangement was that made Belfort say yes to being interviewed. Whether or not he was a 'victim' in that circumstance is a matter for viewers to decide. I'd suggest he was delusional if he wasn't expecting questions to be asked in the vein they were. Regardless, preparation for all possibilities when it comes to media interviews is essential, not least for a man who says he's remorseful but whose behaviours, actions, and tone suggest otherwise.

While my interview topic for the national television program was nowhere near as contentious, and I'd received the questions from the producer and was well-prepared, it had been years since I'd sat in a TV studio, with the bright lights blaring, an 'ear bug' in my ear so I could hear audio, staring down the barrel of a camera waiting to be asked the first question by my interviewers, who were interstate, and who I couldn't see.

I felt the usual mix of nerves and excitement, and the focus it requires to be 'on' and live to air. I was also reminded of how confronting and intimidating it is for people who aren't regular recipients of media attention. TV studios are filled with technical gear, rigging, ladders, cables, lights and reflectors, and large cameras. I could see myself on a TV monitor, but couldn't see the people who were interviewing me. I couldn't look at the monitor during the interview, because I needed to look at the camera. It's a strange environment, and I had to call on my past experiences to know what to do and when. I feel for anyone who's put in that sort of position for the first time. The studio guys will get you a plastic cup of water and tell you where to look, but they aren't always so great at giving you all the information you need, such as ensuring you don't take your eyes off the camera, even if you don't know whether you're being shown on TV for the entire interview or not.

The first question was easy enough to answer, and then the interview took a direction I didn't expect, and for which I hadn't prepared. I wasn't asked any of the questions the producer had given me. Not a single one.

I know that my interviewers weren't trying to make my life difficult. They simply had their own agenda, regardless of what the producer had told and given them—and me—and they were more interested in that. As an ex-journo, I get it.

I winged my way through the interview. I called on information I'd stored away and didn't even know I knew. I got away with it.

I called on my many years of being put under pressure on live TV and radio, with technical glitches and some serious stuff-ups too, that only occasionally—fortunately—left me looking stupid, and not wanting to go back and do it ever again. I called on my Wise Talk Brand, my voice, my credibility, my presence, my knowledge of how to give the media what they want, and all manner of qualities I needed in those few minutes on air. When the interview was over, I breathed a very deep sigh of relief.

No-one was any wiser. I was thanked for doing a great job. When I told people that I'd been asked questions I hadn't expected, and to which I was unsure of the answer, no-one believed me, saying I was so professional and amazing and, and, and ... it was all good. And I know they were telling the truth. Given my media presenting background, I'm what journos call 'good talent'. I also know that that interview was a close shave, and a reminder that, despite my extensive media presenting experience, it would be wise to be much better prepared next time.

Your first step in preparing for a media interview is to focus on the type of presence you want to exude, and to create your Wise Talk Brand for the particular situation.

How do you want to be perceived? What are the actions required for you to be perceived that way? What's the tone required for you to be perceived the way you want to be? Be purposeful.

If there's been a crisis, for example, and two staff members have been killed in a company fire, how do you want to be seen? As someone who's more concerned about sharing facts about the incident and refusing to answer questions that might implicate your company for potential wrong doing, or as a leader who shows genuine care in putting people first, on focusing and connecting with what matters most to your audience?

In other words, do you want to be perceived as cagey and defensive, or as a human being with a heart, and a vision?

Amid the stress of such a situation—not just dealing with the crisis but also the media, with their unique and relentless demands—it's easy to forget what's important to a public audience, and that they carry an enormous amount of power.

Consider next the second tenet of the Wise Talk Leadership Communication Method: Personal.

Remind yourself of what it means to be genuine, to speak with integrity. What will you say to connect with your audience? How will you say it? How will you cultivate trust? This doesn't require overthinking. Remember: it's not about faking it. This is about being aligned, and being yourself, at your best.

Human beings don't need to fake empathy, but if you're worried that doing so might implicate you somehow, then you won't be congruent when you speak.

Connection means reminding yourself of what it means to be human, that real people make up every audience, and it's your job to not only use words they easily understand, but to move them. It's essential that you're clear about the importance of this, and put a premium on connection.

Lastly, what will it take to lead in the media interview? What will it take when the subject is touchy at best, and dire at worst? What will it take to focus less on information and more on inspiration? What will it take to be visionary? How will you operate as a change agent? How will you inspire others to alter their thoughts, perspectives, or actions?

Most organisations are insular. They live and breathe what

they do every day and forget that the outside world probably has a different perspective. They know their facts and figures, their specific technologies, and their area of specialty. But try sharing all of that in a media interview and most of it will fall on deaf ears for the majority of public listeners. It's a skill to step outside your usual world and consider your audience, and how best to not only connect with them, but inspire them too.

Going back to the example of two staff members being killed in the fire at work, what would it take to be visionary and inspire your audience?

I've seen many a spokesperson say all the right things, such as "it's a terrible accident that's happened" and "it will be investigated" and "our priority is ensuring safety for our staff." Their messages were okay, they knew how to take charge of the interview and not buy in to questions that weren't in their organisation's best interests. But there was something crucial missing. Most of those spokespeople showed little heart when they spoke. They were too concerned about not saying the wrong thing.

If you were a parent whose child had been killed in an accident, you'd most likely say, 'it's a terrible thing that's happened' with deep and obvious sadness, certainly with heart. Your words would be congruent with your feelings and purpose, as they need to be in a media interview too. I'm not suggesting you burst into tears. What I am saying is that you need to be genuine.

There's an opportunity to talk about your vision for your organisation—or even better, your industry, as that shows your care and concern across a broader sphere—and how that might relate to the tragedy, as appropriate. Perhaps what's happened has reinforced your vision on a whole new level, and you can use that to rally the troops during a very testing time. Perhaps what's occurred has caused you to revisit or add something new to your vision. Talk about that.

Vision helps people figure out what's important, especially amidst chaos. As a leader, you're the holder and carrier of vision. Make sure you share it.

Remember, being inspiring comes from being bold, taking a stand, making a declaration, and being interesting. Boring, black-and-white and middle of the road won't cut it. Tell us in a way that makes us want more. Tell us in a way that makes us want to do something about it too. Tell us in a way that makes us care.

The media have the power to make or break careers and companies. As a reporter for a number one rating weeknight current affairs program, time and again I covered a story about a fledgling business which really did become an overnight success thanks to our coverage. In our office, we always knew which stories would get the phone ringing, and stood by to answer call after call as soon as the story aired. The switchboard would jam each time. People wanted the phone number for the business featured in the story so they could get a piece of the action and spend their dollars as soon as possible.

On the flip side, the demise of leaders and companies exposed for wrongdoing, or even the suggestion of it, was just as quick. Interviewees who were obviously nervous, ill-prepared, and succumbed to a reporter's tough questions paid a serious price with their reputation and their company's bottom line.

You can't afford to get it wrong with the media.

Now that you've worked out your Wise Talk Brand for your particular situation, here are 35 practical and essential Wise Talk Media Tips for handling media interviews, from the basic to the complex, the ordinary to the visionary.

CHAPTER 3:

WISE TALK MEDIA TIPS 1-5

WISE TALK MEDIA TIP 1 – KNOW WHAT YOU'RE DEALING WITH

Let's play a game. You might remember this from when you were a child. It's called *Who am I?*

I'm lazy, in a hurry, expect people to drop everything and meet my demands, love pushing boundaries, and won't take *no* for an answer. Who am I?

Great guess! Yes, I'm a journalist!

I might have also added that I want the lead story, which is on the front page of the newspaper, or the first in a TV or radio news bulletin. I have a deadline to meet, and I want everyone involved to cooperate with me. I don't have time for people who mess around or get in my way. I want to do a great job. I'm extremely competitive. I want information in my story that no reporter from another news outlet will have.

Game over.

You need to know what you're dealing with, to understand the nature of the beast, so to speak.

Newsrooms these days are diminishing. Reporters don't have as much time as they'd love to research stories. They're not experts. I repeat, journalists are not experts. You need to remember that you'll always know more about the interview topic than they do.

Reporters are in a hurry. They have daily deadlines. For a radio journalist, that deadline might be just five or ten minutes away.

A dream interviewee for a journalist is one who returns calls quickly and makes an effort to cooperate. That might mean dropping what you're doing to accommodate a journalist's request, and making yourself available in an hour's time for an interview.

A nightmare interviewee is one who doesn't return calls, is rarely available, or has her communications department respond three days later. That's when you hear comments in an article or broadcast story that sound like this: '... *was unavailable for comment*'.

Consider the message that sends. Also consider that you get back what you give. It makes for poor relationship building, and nigh on impossible to get a run in the media when you want coverage for you or your organisation's wonderful achievement. There's no such thing as a free lunch, nor free media attention.

I've seen countless organisations with large communications departments play a defensive game with the media, telling themselves there's no point buying into, or adding to, the (usually negative) stories being told about them. They've kept quiet and aloof, all the while giving off an air of superiority amid their shroud of secrecy.

They've done so at their peril, and created a poor reputation that continually feeds itself without their input. Doing something controversial in the community? Open your mind and your doors, grab our hand and take us with you, show us the way, walk a mile in our shoes and try to understand why we feel the way we do. Then make an effort to communicate with us on our level, and keep in touch.

Knowledge is power. Connection is gold. For your organisation, and for the public.

Remember too that the media need to get a story to air. If you won't provide a comment, they'll look elsewhere, even if it means talking to someone who lives in the street where the police raid on the warehouse just happened. That person will speculate. That's just what people do, and it's unlikely it will be in your favour. It's always better that we hear from you.

WISE TALK MEDIA TIP 2 - DON'T FEED US MORE JUNK FOOD

LOAVES AND FISHES

This is not the age of information. This is not the age of information.

Forget the news, and the radio, and the blurred screen.

This is the time of loaves and fishes.

People are hungry, and one good word is bread for a thousand.

— David Whyte

Society is fed a steady diet of stodgy fear. Turn on the nightly news and check out the rundown of stories and the messages they're feeding us:

- New taxes (Message: *we won't be able to afford it, life is getting harder*)
- School in lockdown (Message: *our children, our streets, our lives aren't safe*)
- A priest caught with child porn (Message: *we can't trust anyone these days*)
- A man admits murdering a debt collector (Message: *it's scary what happens in the world, what if that happened in our street? To someone we love?*)

I didn't make up that list. I took it straight from a 6pm commercial TV news bulletin. Everywhere you look, fear-filled messages are getting louder and louder, amidst rants and raves, especially on social media.

Facebook admitted it conducted an Emotion Manipulation study, by tweaking the news feeds of nearly 700-thousand users to show a disproportionate number of negative or positive statuses for one week. The conclusion reached by the study was that the emotions of others on your news feed affects your mood.

As is increasingly becoming common practice, Facebook researchers didn't inform users they were manipulating their news feeds. Legally, they are allowed to do what they did. Regardless, it sparked outrage amongst a growing community becoming more and more disenchanted and angry about the power Facebook holds in its very sticky hands.

As a leader, will you also feed us a diet of junk food when you're given the opportunity to speak to us via the media?

You can't sugar coat it. Bad news is bad news. But you can share your vision, know what common ground you share with your audience to create connection, and relay the good news. What's the way out? What can be done? How can we do this together?

Remember, people are hungry. They long for leaders they can trust.

What's the one good word you'll share?

WISE TALK MEDIA TIP 3 – NAIL THE ESSENTIALS

I want to give you a list of the basic dos and don'ts that matter.

I call them basic, although I want you to understand that what I'm giving you matters immensely when it comes to dealing with the media. It could be the difference between digging yourself a very deep hole and ensuring journalists do their best to stay away from you—and choose someone else to interview next time—or being the number one choice in your industry as a leader who's considered 'great talent'.

One of my tactics as a journalist was always to ask, at the end of every interview, this question: *Is there anything else you want to add?*

Those eight words that sounded innocent enough were usually swooped on by interviewees, who thought they were being given the chance to finally say what they really wanted to say.

I started asking the question innocently enough because there may well have been something I missed. Quickly, I learned that the majority of people, when given free reign, would divulge all sorts of information that would have been better kept to themselves. It was a win for me. It's a trap for you.

Despite people preparing their messages before the interview, human nature took over … and so many people fell into it.

Take note of my list of the basic essentials:

- Arrive at an interview with prepared 'grabs' or sound

bites, intriguing stories, anecdotes, quotes and statistics that pack a punch

- Be extremely well prepared. Winging it won't cut it
- Be interesting to listen to

- Know the latest news affecting your industry and be ready to comment about it
- Don't ramble. The more you say, they more likely you'll dig a hole for yourself. Droning diminishes your presence
- When given the opportunity to say whatever you like, don't
- Communicate precisely. Get to your point and stick to it
- Be accurate and honest. Put integrity first
- Be bold and own what you stand for
- Show enthusiasm. Be excited when you're sharing greatnews. Smile.
- Be real

WISE TALK MEDIA TIP 4 - IT'S NOT ABOUT YOU

What do you need to get out of the interview?
What would your audience find helpful?

No-one ever asked me these questions when I was a reporter. I wish someone had. It would not only have made my life easier, it would have endeared me to the person asking, and put him at the top of my list to interview again.

It would have made me want to build our relationship. And it likely would have meant more free airtime for him, a bigger stage, and more opportunities to build his reputation and brand.

One of my clients does all her own PR. She's a whizz at building relationships and showing gratitude where it's due. She gives. She doesn't manipulate or bribe though—there's a difference.

She gets an extraordinary amount of media coverage for her business—if you were to put a figure on it, it would easily be worth hundreds of thousands of dollars by now.

She knows that reporters are people, too. They respond to those who show a genuine interest in them, and make an effort to connect.

The last time I was featured in a newspaper article, I emailed the journalist to thank her, not just for the opportunity, but also for her accuracy and integrity. She was blown away by such a small sentiment.

Remember, most people are scared, or at the very least, suspicious of reporters. They know that. They know they're near the top of the list of the most distrusted professions, along with politicians, psychics, real estate agents and religious ministers.

Treat journalists well, and ask how best you can help them do their job.

It's a wise investment that will pay dividends.

WISE TALK MEDIA TIP 5: DON'T TALK TO THE MEDIA

Yes, I did mean to write that. Don't talk to the media.

The media are your messengers, not your audience. First and foremost, remember to focus on your audience and how what you have to say is relevant to them.

I'll never forget interviewing countless numbers of police officers when I was a young journalist. In my first job, during the radio breakfast shift, it was common to ring the police media department around five am to find out if anything of interest had happened overnight. Those police officers were trained to simply share the facts, and somehow had forgotten what it meant to be a human, let alone speak like one.

They'd give statements like this: *At 0430 hours a suspect was detained after a high-speed chase in the northern suburbs. Another suspect decamped by foot in an easterly direction. He's described as Caucasian, of stocky build, and was wearing a black balaclava.*

When I first started making phone calls to the police media department and listened to those statements, I'd giggle. I couldn't believe that anyone would speak that way. Connection? Hardly.

But it's no different when CEOs of organisations with complex issues delve down into numbers and figures and processes that most of us don't understand, nor care about.

It's widely accepted that, in order to ensure what you're talking about is understood, you need to use language a thirteen or fourteen-year-old would understand.

I'm not suggesting you 'dumb it down'. But no-one wins a prize for using big words and dosing up conversations with corporate jargon. Government speak and acronyms don't belong in media interviews, either. Keep it simple.

If you think your audience is different, perhaps more sophisticated, I'm here to tell you that's not true.

Audiences want to know how what you're saying affects them, and if not them directly, then others in the community.

I'm asking you to be inclusive. I'm asking you to be respectful and kind. I'm asking you to consider that, most likely, most people in your audience don't know all the background to what you're saying.

Chances are your potential clients and customers are in your audience. If you're a doctor, use bedside patient language, not medico-speak. If you head a corporate organisation, use customer or client-speak.

It's the first step in creating connection. It matters enormously.

CHAPTER 4:

WISE TALK MEDIA TIPS 6-10

WISE TALK MEDIA TIP 6 – GO IN

There's a former state premier who's renowned for placing both hands in front of him, as if he were resting them in his lap, and then bringing them up to belly height. When he speaks, his hands go up and down almost in train with his thoughts. Back in the day, us journos knew he was constantly trying to remember what to say next. With a glazed look in his eyes, he'd stare down the barrel of the TV cameras, never looking once at the reporters who asked him the questions. He was focused fair and square on remembering his messages.

It became a focus of mine to try to engage politicians in ordinary conversations. Except for a couple, it was an impossible feat. They were so highly trained to behave like ... well, politicians. And they knew the potential costs of getting it wrong.

People who are trying so hard to remember their messages, and what to say and what not to say, are disconnected from themselves and us, their audience. We feel it. We know it. And we don't trust them.

The best way to ensure that your message is delivered the right way is to internalise it.

What you're talking about needs to:

- Matter to you
- Be meaningful

When it is, you'll naturally speak with enthusiasm and passion, empathy and sadness, concern and anger—as appropriate.

When it isn't, then you shouldn't be talking about it. Get someone else who cares to do the interview for you.

WISE TALK MEDIA TIP 7 - MASTER MESSAGE MAKING

Most media trainers tell you you need to prepare your key messages before an interview. Key messages form the most important information you'll communicate during your interview with a reporter.

The question is, what's a key message? A bullet point? A talking point? Words that are heavy on spin and light on truth?

The problem with bullet points and talking points is that you're giving yourself a licence to ad lib. That's dangerous. When you wing it, you're in danger of sinking the ship.

The best way to deal with this, and prepare for the interview, is to define three key areas you want to talk about. Create a few sentences that are quotable.

Those sentences need to include your key messages. Then, internalise and learn them.

Consider your conversation as a tree, with three branches. I call it the Wise Talk Tree. You need a tree trunk message made up of two sentences that not only anchor the conversation, but sum up what you want to say. The first sentence and message incorporate your vision, value, mission and belief.

The second sentence points to the three key areas that you're prepared to talk about.

Then come up with two more sentences for each of the three branches. They need to be quotable, and add a few more facts, as well as point to other important areas you want to talk about.

This is a technique that takes some time to master, but can be taught in half a day. For now, visualise a tree with a large trunk and three large branches, then add three limbs to each of the branches. Then add three twigs to each of the limbs. Then add three leaves to each of the twigs. If it helps, draw a picture.

The leaves represent detail, while the trunk and three branches symbolise the basic facts and main points.

You make interviews easy when you populate your tree with quotable sentences that you internalise and remember, because your tree has created a conversation and tells a story.

This takes preparation, and I'm trusting that's not a surprise to you. An interview is serious business, potentially a deal maker or breaker.

I've known CEOs who blocked aside a full day to prepare for their appearance on a national TV show. They're smart.

WISE TALK MEDIA TIP 8 – CONTROL THE INTERVIEW

Most people go into an interview wondering what they'll be asked. And then, while they're answering one question, they're thinking about what will come next.

It makes not only for distraction, but a sheer lack of presence. It also makes it difficult to focus on what you're doing, and do a great job.

I have a confession to make. When I was a news reporter, I often didn't know which question I'd ask next. I usually didn't show up to an interview with a list of questions already prepared—I'd usually had little time to do much research, and after a while, I learned that most of the questions I needed to ask were standard in plenty of situations.

When I was working in current affairs, and my stories were four to five times longer than news stories, I did show up with specific questions, both because I'd had more time to prepare and required a lot more information.

For an average news interview, you can expect the journalist to make up questions on the spot, once the interview begins.

It's common practice to ask a few 'soft' questions to help you relax, and then get tougher, and possibly negative, as the interview progresses.

Most people don't realise that it's possible to take charge and control the interview. You can. Here's what you need to know:

What you say in an answer will usually be the basis of the next question a reporter asks you.

Journalists are skilled at mirroring your language. For example, if the last words in your answer are, ' … we expect production to increase dramatically next year to keep up with demand', what do you think the next question will be? The reporter will likely ask, 'What is the demand likely to be next year'?

The trick for you is to craft answers in a way that makes the journalist want to know more, and ask a follow up question. It's a form of teasing, in a way, that allows you to control the interview and the questions. The reporter simply follows along, and you're also making her life easy, because she doesn't really have to think about her next question.

Interviews can take much longer than they need to if you're giving answers that don't satisfy a journalist's needs. You might have provided all the facts required, but reporters want a quote they can use in the story. The faster you provide one or two great quotes, the sooner the interview will be over.

With people who were great talent, I remember some interviews taking just a couple of minutes. I sometimes only needed to ask three or four questions. I knew what I wanted, and when I received it, there was no point wasting time asking more questions.

It is possible to control an interview when you know how.

WISE TALK TIP 9 - FORGET ABOUT BODY LANGUAGE

I'm about to contradict what most media trainers will tell you. In truth, there are very few body language techniques you need to know, even for TV interviews.

That's because, once you've worked out your Wise Talk Brand and are aligned with it, you're more than halfway there. You'll likely be open to the interview experience, and not dealing with worrying thoughts. If they do come up, simply notice them and then go back to your Wise Talk Brand statement. Then you'll also have body language that's naturally open rather than defensive.

I can't tell you how many times I've interviewed people who didn't want to be there, expected me to give them a hard time, thought they were superior, were extremely nervous, and were easily angered by questions they didn't want to answer.

It was no skin off my nose. I didn't need them to like me or be happy with me. I just had to get the interview and get my story to air that night. But guess what? Everything they were thinking and feeling was being beamed to audiences of 200-thousand plus, in the days before pay TV and the burgeoning online community.

The angry stares. The fast talking. The glares and rolling eyes of condescension. The red blotchiness of discomfort at being in the spotlight. The talking over me to cut me off. The higher tones of voice to show annoyance. The frowns. All of it was on show.

Those people who are open, on the other hand, and genuinely want to connect with their audiences, regardless of the story, and are clear about their Wise Talk Brand statement, present themselves not only as confident and authoritative, but genuine and trustworthy too.

Here are a few simple body language techniques that can be helpful for TV interviews:

- Sit up straight in your chair
- Put both feet on the floor, rather than crossing your legs. This will help you to feel grounded, and you'll be less likely to move around on your chair
- If you're being interviewed standing up, make sure you stand still and place your feet shoulder-width apart
- Maintain eye contact with your interviewer

For radio and phone interviews, none of that matters. However, it's always grounding and calming to ensure that you have both feet firmly on the floor.

WISE TALK MEDIA TIP 10 – PLAY YOUR OWN GAME

Normal conversations are about rapport. There's give and take. Most of us naturally mirror the body language of those to whom we're speaking as a way of connecting. We build rapport by being kind and usually, when we're asked questions, we do our best to answer them.

So what happens during a media interview when you're asked a question you don't want to answer, or don't know how best to answer?

One of the most common pitfalls during a media interview is that interviewees give all their power to the journalist. It's easy to do, especially if there's a TV camera in your face and bright lights. A media conference can be even more intimidating, with several journalists vying to ask questions all at once.

What most people forget is that they're being interviewed because they're experts in their field.

You know more than the reporter. You are the expert in your role, organisation or perhaps industry. A journalist will never know more than you do about your topic. *Never*.

What most people also forget is that they have an enormous amount of power when given the opportunity to be interviewed by the media. How else can your message reach such a large audience?

With more cost cutting, newsrooms are shrinking, and there are a growing number of young, inexperienced journalists in some news organisations in particular. That can be a good thing and a very bad thing.

For you, as the expert, it's your job to call the shots in an interview. It's your job to take charge and play it on your terms. You always need to behave with integrity and speak the truth. Be honest. But you decide which truths are in the best interests of your audience, and your organisation. You wouldn't lay all your cards on the table for your competitors, for example. And why would the majority of your audience be interested anyway?

Remind yourself of your Wise Talk Brand for the particular situation. If it's 'Amicable, Firm & Caring', and you're asked a question you don't want to answer, how would you handle it?

There are words you can use like 'What's important here ...' or 'What we need to focus on ...' to steer the interview the way you want it to go. You're under no obligation to answer a question you don't want to answer, but you'll need to speak with a tone of voice that's amicable, firm, and caring.

It's a technique you use when you're asked a negative question. You block it and bridge to something positive, then hook the reporter with new information. This can distract the journalist and take the interview in a more positive direction.

On the other hand, it can be dangerous because it's so overt it can make it look as though you have something to hide. You might be lucky to encounter a journalist who lets you get away with it, but you also run the risk of making the reporter hostile and aggressive.

The best approach is to answer with a strong key message that gives enough information to answer the question without exposing vulnerabilities, to satisfy your interviewer. Then use a bridge to more positive information that contains a story, fact, or example that's so interesting the reporter will want to pursue a new line of questioning.

It takes role-playing to master this technique, ideally on camera.

After years of interviewing people, I've picked up how to do this myself, usually without even thinking about it. When my first book was released, I was interviewed live for forty-five minutes on an American radio station's book show. It was 6am for me, and I was doing my best to be awake. Afterwards, when I was emailed a copy of the interview, I listened and noticed that I didn't answer a lot of the questions the way they were intended. I acknowledged them and used one of my key messages, then just went on to say what I wanted to say.

Politicians overtly do it all the time, hardly acknowledging the question at all. It's how they handle just about every question, which is a source of great frustration for reporters.

Police officers do it too. Please don't do that yourself, unless your Brand is 'Distant, Self-Serving & Distrustful'!

Do take charge, decide what you want to say and what's out of bounds for you, have well-prepared messages on your Wise Talk Tree, and practice, practice, practice.

Journalists believe they're the bastions of truth, and raised on a diet of doubt, they're on a mission to make you prove everything you say.

That sounds dramatic, yet it is the accepted undercurrent. Journalists are fast to believe something negative and take a lot longer to buy into what's being presented as positive.

Do your homework.

CHAPTER 5:

WISE TALK MEDIA TIPS 11-15

WISE TALK MEDIA TIP 11 – DON'T PLAY THE SPECULATION GAME

There's been a serious outbreak of food poisoning traced to the salami your smallgoods factory produces. As the salami is removed from supermarket shelves, and more people require hospital treatment, journalists are having a field day, gathering outside your office door to throw questions at you like this:

- How much worse could it get?
- What's the worst that could happen here?
- What if people die?
- Will you be forced to never produce that product again?
- Will you be forced to shut down operations?
- Will you close your doors for good?

Reporters love speculating. They want to get a great story. They'd be over the moon if you bought into their speculation and dropped a 'yes' here and there, confirming their questions— which, at times, can be ridiculous.

Watch out for speculative questions. If you go down the path of answering them, you'll make the story bigger than it is. That's not what you want. Your job is to take charge, extinguish the flames, and be the voice of reason and trust.

Try these responses:

- 'I can't speculate on that, but what I can tell you is …'
- 'It's not appropriate for me to speculate about that, but what I can say is …'

Those responses will take the reporter back to one of your key messages and a fact you've previously confirmed.

Sometimes you might be asked to speak for someone else too. If so, you can say, 'I can't speak for them, but what I can tell you is …'

Often journalists don't have their facts straight before they interview you. It's your job to set them straight. Don't be afraid to do that. You can simply say that a fact in one of the reporter's questions wasn't correct, and go ahead and correct it.

Don't relinquish control. Remember, you're in charge of the interview. This is your moment of power.

WISE TALK TIP 12 - PRACTICE, PRACTICE, PRACTICE

You might have an hour's notice. Maybe just a few minutes. Regardless, you need to practice before a media interview, even if it's a good news story. Winging it is never wise.

What you think you want to say, what you plan to say, and what comes out of your mouth when you start talking are usually remarkably different.

Even if you just have five or ten minutes, your best bet is to ask someone to ask you a few questions. Make sure you nail your opening lines to command your audience's attention. Make sure there are no stutters or stumbles, and definitely no rambling.

Go through the process at least twice. Invest not just in getting it right, but excelling.

Remember, if you fail to deliver great quotes and speak with clarity, you risk no coverage at all for your good news story.

What you say, and how you say it, potentially impacts your organisation's bottom line.

Practice.

WISE TALK TIP 13 – BE PREPARED FOR THE TOUGH STUFF

A ten-minute practice session won't cut it when it comes to a very negative news story. If you find yourself in the position of being interviewed by an investigative journalist for an extensive story on a serious current affairs program, or for a major newspaper or magazine piece, you need to prepare like you would for a battle.

One of my clients wisely spent an entire day training to appear on a current affairs program. That was after several sessions of being hammered by his communications team.

The good news about one of these interviews is that you're usually given plenty of notice, and have plenty of time to prepare. To do that, you need to have people—ideally someone from your PR or communications team—play the role of the investigative reporter. You also need to train and practice until you know the answer to every question.

The not so good news is that the journalist might have spent weeks working on the story, digging up all sorts of information.

This is where most people play a guessing game, working out the types of questions they might be asked. Journalists do come with standard questions, but in this scenario, you can bet they're not planning a good news story and that they've done a lot more homework than a reporter who covers the daily news.

Journalists don't want to tell you exactly what they want to talk to you about, either. They'll likely be a little cagey and vague, wanting to hook you with their brilliant line of questioning based on discovering information they're hoping you don't know they know. They think that if they catch you off guard, you'll be more honest and less likely to sell them spin.

You have every right to ask a reporter more questions than you answer, especially when you agree to take part in an interview. If you have a communications team, this is their job. Not enough people do this, and it can be a game changer in controlling the interview.

It's important to listen very carefully to what the reporter tells you, and what he doesn't. Become an expert at reading between the lines.

You can ask:

- 'Tell me what prompted you to investigate this story'?
- 'What do you want your audience to take away from the story'?
- 'Who else have you talked to? Who else do you plan to interview'?
- 'What have those people told you so far'?

There are many more questions you can and should ask, and I save them for my clients. After all, printing them here would be letting the media in on our secrets.

In my twenty years as a journalist, I don't remember ever being extensively questioned. People very easily said 'yes' to my requests for interviews, and I always approached them with a clear intention that they would.

Use this technique and you'll not only be ahead of the pack, but you'll be so well-prepared that you'll nail the interview.

Once you've carried out your extensive questioning, step into the shoes of the journalist and write the story the way you think the journalist would, based on what he said and didn't say. Be cynical. Be brutal. Then share the story with your team to get their buy-in on the importance of being fully media-trained and prepared for the interview.

Go through the story. Identify facts and assumptions, the source of the story, and what you know about the people the reporter has already spoken to and from whom he's gleaned information. Come up with a long list of questions you think you might be asked. Be tough, because the questions no doubt will be.

Research the true answers to each question. Gather supportive background material. Write the answers to every question. Make sure they're quotable and written in the Wise Talk Tree I shared with you in Tip 7.

Training for this requires role-playing interviews, ideally on camera, until you have every question covered and every answer is seamless. This is serious. There are heavy costs for getting it wrong in the real interview, including an impact on your business and bottom line.

I'm often asked whether it's possible to know every question you'll be asked. With this type of intensive preparation, it is.

There's nothing more satisfying than to walk away from a high-stakes interview knowing you nailed it.

WISE TALK TIP 14 — TURN AROUND NEGATIVE QUESTIONS

The reality is that most news is negative because it's usually about change, disaster, or tragedy. If there's good news, it's mostly tucked away at the end of a news bulletin, and rarely makes the front page of the newspaper.

When I was working for a commercial current affairs program, the other two reporters in the office loved nothing more than to 'kick down doors'. They revelled in chasing crooks, exposing filthy houses inhabited by 'neighbours from hell', and using the hidden 'sneaky' camera to try to catch people in the act of doing dodgy things.

Someone had to do the 'soft' stories, which were mostly frowned upon by the journalists who considered themselves 'serious'. I had a penchant for those so-called soft stories, mostly because I didn't feel comfortable 'exposing' people for what were often innocent mistakes, yet had the capacity to seriously harm their businesses. I also believed that audiences were more likely to connect with what were called, funnily enough, 'human interest stories' (if the other stories weren't of human interest, I wondered why we ran them at all—but no-one could seem to answer that question).

I felt that something positive amongst all the negativity was a good thing, too. I wish the news didn't purvey such fear. But it won't change.

However, you can change the way you deal with it, so that you don't need to perpetuate fear and harm your own reputation, as well as that of your organisation, by falling for negative questions.

Here's what to do:

- Listen to how questions are phrased. Is it a negative question?
- If it is, choose not to directly answer it. You're under no obligation to do that
- Work out whether the question could be phrased in a more positive way, and if it can, ask yourself the positive question in your mind
- Answer the question using a positive answer that responds to the positive question you created in your mind

All this takes place in a split second or two. You can practice this in your every day conversations to make it second nature.

I'm reminded of a story *60 Minutes* ran about petroleum giant BP spilling millions of litres of crude oil into the Gulf of Mexico. It was the worst offshore oil disaster in US history.

A chemical dispersant was sprayed on the spill to break it up, and while the oil did disappear, people started getting sick— and some started dying.

A *60 Minutes* reporter interviewed the Chief Executive of the National Offshore Petroleum Safety and Environmental Management Authority, Jane Cutler. Her job is to regulate all oil platforms, and she told *60 Minutes* that the Authority must approve the use of any dispersants. An oil rig that had just reopened was mentioned, in particular its oil spill emergency response plan that had been approved, which included the use of the dispersants used in the Gulf of Mexico disaster.

Clearly uncomfortable with being interviewed, Jane Cutler struggled more and more as the questions grew tougher. She looked like a deer caught in headlights as though she knew she was doomed. She chose not to answer questions, and asked for time to read through documents the reporter had on hand, saying she hadn't seen them and would need to read them to comment. She took the documents and walked out of the room.

It was excruciating to watch this interviewee's discomfort and clear lack of preparation. She was kidding herself if she wasn't expecting to be grilled. If she'd been professionally trained and ready, she would have been able to turn the negative questions around.

You *will* be asked negative questions by a journalist. I repeat, *you will be asked negative questions.*

Some of the questions Jane Cutler was asked were:

- 'Do you know how safe or how toxic these dispersants are'?
- 'What guarantees have they given you about how they will safely handle an oil spill if it happened again'?
- 'Are you aware that those two dispersants are banned in eighteen countries'?

The reporter was implying, with that last question, that Jane

Cutler's organisation hadn't been doing its job properly. The eerie background music became louder, and Jane Cutler was left to suffer the damage to her own reputation and that of her organisation. Ouch.

As a leader, it was Jane Cutler's job to share her vision, assure us, and make us trust her. That didn't happen.

Taking the last question as an example, if she'd used the technique of turning a negative question into a positive one, the question behind the question was: 'If there's an oil spill, will we suffer the same fate in Australia as the Gulf of Mexico?'

Could that be turned into a positive question? Yes. A positive question would have been: 'People in the community are afraid there'll be another oil spill and people will die. What assurances can you give that companies will operate in a safe manner?'

Then, the positive answer would have been: 'For us to approve contingency plans, there's a strict process that's adhered to, and that has taken place. I'll explain what we do to ensure safety and prevent oil spills'.

This is a skill that takes practice, and not just when you know you have an interview coming up. You can incorporate it into your daily conversations. If you choose to do that, you'll notice that people start to respond differently towards you. People will respect and trust you more. They'll look to you as a leader they want to follow. Your presence will become more powerful.

Try it for a month and track the changes. You'll be surprised.

WISE TALK MEDIA TIP 15 – PASSION WINS THE DAY

Passion is underestimated and it's a powerful tool.

As a visionary leader, passion is something that's easy for you to access. When you can use great quotes and express them passionately, you'll control the direction of a media story.

Politicians, in particular, are great at coming up with memorable quotes but don't always excel in delivering them. If you're not naturally a fiery and charismatic character, and you lean more towards details, you might need to dig deep to internalise your message and deliver it with meaning, heart, and passion.

Add emotion and passion to be bold, stand out, and become memorable.

One of my clients, an activist, has created a worldwide movement to encourage and celebrate positive body image. Within eighteen months she created a social media community of nearly 60,000 followers, and she's enjoyed extensive traditional media coverage around Australia, the US and the UK. She's incredibly passionate when she speaks, provides great quotes, and has made herself irresistible to the media because she knows how to give them what they want.

She's exceptional talent. Several media outlets have asked her back time and again.

Passion sells you, what you stand for, and your organisation. If you're not the person for this job, select a different spokesperson who has the goods. Passion is crucial to inspire followership.

CHAPTER 6:

WISE TALK MEDIA TIPS 16-20

WISE TALK MEDIA TIP 16 – EVERYTHING'S ON THE RECORD

Theoretically, only what's recorded in a conversation with a journalist is on the record. Theoretically, a journalist should tell you when something is on or off the record.

Realistically, treat any conversation with a journalist as though it's on the record. Sometimes cameramen are recording what you're saying after the interview is over. The integrity of a reporter who uses that as part of the story might well be questionable, but it does happen. In any case, treat everything as if it's on the record and there won't be a problem.

If you're asked to speak off the record, don't do it.

Even if your words aren't used directly in a quote in the story, for example, they'll be used in some way. The story might say, 'A confidential source tells us ...' and divulge the information. Anyone close enough to the topic is likely to trace the information back to you, and that damages your reputation.

A reporter might ask you to provide background information, and you might see that as off the record. Don't.

Be ethical.

WISE TALK MEDIA TIP 17 – TAKE SOCIAL MEDIA SERIOUSLY

I know this isn't easy to do when news feeds on Facebook are filled with questions about how to tie a bow tie, quizzes to work out the story behind your date of birth and what your Game of Thrones name is, prompts to share the first word you find in a grid, the difference between the health of plants grown in microwaved water versus purified water, the latest natural weight loss drug that Nicole Kidman used, celebrity tattoo fails, and photos of the worst hair cuts.

Self-ordained journalists on the internet have changed the face of the media. Anyone can have a say these days, and just about everyone does. Social media outlets have given a voice to the masses. And a lot of the time, what they're saying is scary.

People can post online comments in such a wide variety of forums. It makes the world a frightening place for those concerned about managing their reputation.

Social media tools have given us all the opportunity to post something in a matter of seconds. They've also provided the opportunity for information to go viral, and be shared with more people than ever before. What once might have had a run only in a local newspaper and be forgotten about the next day might now reach millions of people across the entire world and keep on spreading for weeks and weeks.

My client I mentioned in Tip 15 has smartly used social media to build her profile and campaign. A few months into her project, one of her posts went viral and reached millions of people in just a couple of weeks. That activity led to her being flown interstate to be interviewed on a national TV breakfast show. Her audience is spread across the world, and she's used them to build a strong community who've supported her—and done a lot of the work for her—to raise more than 330-thousand dollars to produce a documentary. That's the power of social media being used for good.

Let's face it: there's no other form of media with the capacity to go viral on a worldwide scale. Never before has the world been so connected.

You run into trouble, though, when your public actions that aren't admirable are photographed or recorded on video and posted to the web. As I write this, the first thought that comes to mind is the Australian rugby player who was kicked off his team after a photo of him urinating into his own mouth was posted online.

You also run into trouble when your reputation is attacked on social media sites and blogs. I cringe when I see negative and irate comments about companies' poor service shouted across Facebook and Twitter news feeds, and people keep adding their own gripe. It's the type of advertising no-one wants, and it's impossible to control.

I was intrigued by a new Facebook page paying tribute to a convicted criminal who'd been on the run for two weeks, was discovered holed up inside a city brothel, and caused city streets to be placed in lockdown before he shot himself inside the brothel. The page went online within hours of his death, and I watched the number of 'likes' grow by the hundreds, by the minute. Comments were from friends, family and those who despised him, and ranged from sincere sentiments to arguments amongst those posting. Littered with swear words and nasty attacks, I could only begin to imagine what a field day the police were having as they identified the criminal's associates. The sheer lack of concern, and dare I say intelligence, about what was being sprayed across the page saddened me. It's more fuel for the negative fires being stoked online everywhere.

The third way you run into trouble online is when you take part in discussions and don't do a great job at communicating.

Email isn't safe either. A guy I know and used to work with in the media wrote an email to a TV presenter making disparaging comments about her hair, make-up and the way she was dressed. She chose to respond by sharing the comments in a newspaper column that then ended up going viral on social media. She also mentioned the name of person who'd written them. When I read the article, I couldn't help but email my old colleague and ask him what on earth he was thinking. He said he didn't mean the comments in the vein they were taken, and admitted he was a "silly old fool." I felt for him. An email he thought he'd shared privately ended up all over the internet.

It's so easy to instantly air thoughts and opinions these days. It's so easy to speak before you think, make a serious mistake, and have a massive audience hear or see it.

These sorts of scenarios are enough to make you squirm in

your seat when you read them, especially from professional colleagues:

- Sharing their political or religious views
- Posting inappropriate photos
- Discussing corporate information that shouldn't be shared, even if it's not confidential
- Using social media sites to spam about events
- Updating their statuses so frequently that you wonder whether they're doing any actual work
- Writing a blog that, while it doesn't express the views of your organisation and may well say so, is questionable for its content

When it comes to social media, these are the rules:

- Social media should be treated as seriously as traditional media. Every rule of media training applies to social media
- Be extremely careful about what you say to avoid having your comments taken out of context
- Behave congruently, in private and public
- Use your key messages on blogging and forum platforms

You'll notice I said 'rules', not 'guidelines'.

Stick to them for the sake of your leadership.

WISE TALK MEDIA TIP 18 – TELL THE TRUTH

It seems odd that I need to say this, but people do ask me about whether or not they should tell the truth.

Yes, tell the truth. And also be mindful of what's in the best interests of your organisation to share—or not. That's common sense.

We respect and trust people who tell the truth. We respect and trust people who admit mistakes. We want people to level with us, even though most of us think and feel that rarely happens.

The public are fed up with governments and their opposition counterparts blaming one another for everything that's gone wrong. We're sick of direct answers to questions from the media that go like this: 'Whose fault is it that this has happened'?

We want conscious leaders who appear fearless, are vanguards for the greater good of their organisations and community. We don't want blind followers, but leaders who maintain their integrity, personify loyalty and make tough decisions based on conscience.

We don't want to be told over and over by the Prime Minister, after delivering a tough budget, that election promises weren't broken.

We know promises were broken. We're okay with being told that the problems inherited from the previous government were worse than expected, if that's true, as long as the PM tells us that that's meant he's had to break an election promise, and he's *sorry* about that.

Say the word. Be sincere. It doesn't undermine you. It's not an admission of incompetency. In fact, we trust leaders and forgive them more easily if they admit mistakes and express empathy—in the media, and in our workplaces.

WISE TALK MEDIA TIP 19 – LOOK THE PART

Looks do matter. This is basic, I'm asked about it all the time—and it's important. You need to consider how your audience perceives you. You also need to think about what you wear and whether it's a good match with cameras.

For women: Plain, bold colours work best on camera. Always avoid floral, patterned fabric, and frills. They're distracting, and can flare on camera. They also diminish your authority and presence. Too much jewellery won't serve you either.

For men: If you're someone who wears a suit and tie to work, make sure you wear them for an on-camera interview and photo, to match your role and authority. Basic colours work best, such as black, grey and navy for suits, and plain shirts. On camera, checks and stripes are distracting and can flare.

If you are interviewed away from the office, in a more casual setting, it can work well to lose the tie or the jacket. You need to make the call based on the message you want to send to your audience.

If you find yourself being interviewed in a TV studio, make sure you wear make-up. Yes, as a guy, you need make up, too. The studio lighting is very harsh.

Many TV stations will provide a make-up artist, but not always. Ask the producer when the interview is arranged whether make-up will be provided. If it won't, and you need to do it yourself, wear a lot more than usual. Make sure your make up is two to three times heavier. Men just need foundation.

WISE TALK MEDIA TIP 20 –
MAKE SURE THEY DON'T TAKE YOU OUT OF CONTEXT

I can't tell you how many times I've heard this: 'The journalist took me out of context!' And, 'She didn't use the best part of the interview!'

The truth is, if it were the best part, it would have been used in the story. No-one will leave out the best parts.

So often during media conferences, I remember the talent saying something great—a well-worded, punchy quote—and us journalists all looking at one another and wryly smiling. Reporters recognise a great quote. We all knew we had what we needed, and that we'd be putting the same 'grab' in our TV stories that night. How's that for controlling the interview process! That's what I mean about being great talent. Give reporters the goods and they'll use them.

To try to prevent being taken out of context, make sure you don't give journalists too many facts or too much information. They don't need all the details. They start with a headline, and then add the next main fact. They tell a story that illustrates the most important facts, and the big picture. They don't have time in their bulletins, or space in their newspapers or online, for anything else.

A radio news journalist writes just three to four sentences and then plays an audio grab of ten seconds, if you're lucky. A commercial television news reporter has one minute to one-minute-and-twenty seconds—if she's very lucky—to tell your story. A print reporter is usually telling the story in twelve-to-twenty sentences.

Keep your information simple. There's an art to that if you're particularly detail-oriented. It's why I use the Wise Talk Tree and focus on creating the three most important messages.

Use simple language. Stay away from jargon, buzz words and acronyms. They're easily misunderstood.

Before the interview is over, ask the reporter if he clearly understood everything you said. Do it in a way that doesn't sound condescending. Some journalists will nod in agreement, though, whether they understood or not.

Keep it simple.

CHAPTER 7:

WISE TALK MEDIA TIPS 21-25

WISE TALK MEDIA TIP 21 – PLAY THE JOURNALIST BEFORE EVERY INTERVIEW

When a journalist calls to ask if you're available to do an urgent interview, don't do it on the spot. You need to prepare—and as part of your preparation, you need to ask questions.

You won't want to ask everything listed below. It's the journalist's job to grill *you*, after all, not the other way around. And most reporters will—and should—voluntarily offer some of the information below.

You need to decide which of these questions will support you best in preparing for the interview, and then ask them when you speak to the reporter for the first time:

1. **'What's your name?** Which organisation are you from? Do you cover a particular area (i.e. politics or health)?'** Most reporters will tell you this up front, but if not, you'll know what to ask.

2. **'What's the story you're working on?'** Listen carefully to glean as much information as possible, then, if necessary, ask follow up questions to clarify.

3. **'Is there any particular perspective you have in mind for this story?'** or 'Are you approaching this story from a particular perspective?' It's helpful to know this, so make sure you ask in a tone of genuine interest. If you ask a reporter what his angle is, especially in a way that's condescending, you might get his back up.

4. **'Who else are you interviewing for this story?'**

Depending on the story, many reporters won't want to reveal their hand, but it's worth asking. You'll be able to get a sense of the tone of the story by how the reporter answers this question, as well as whether the other interviewees are supporters or opponents of your cause.

5. **'Where, when, and how?'** If it's for a print interview, is it an in-depth story, front-page news, or a small story near the back of the newspaper? For radio, is it a live interview with talk back or a recorded interview for news that will be edited? Will you do it over the phone or will you be asked to come to the studio? For TV, is it live or recorded? Where does the reporter want to conduct the interview? How long will the interview take? Who will be doing the interview? With answers to these questions, you can prepare *your* answers accordingly.

6. **'What do you need from me?** What else can I provide?' Ask if you can provide videos, photos, graphics, or other documents that will not only add to story—and help you have more input into and influence on the story—but make a journalist's day easier. TV journos love getting fresh vision via a video, and anything else that will add to how their stories look on air. People who understand this really are a journalist's dream. Offer to help in this way and watch your relationship with the media flourish.

7. **'When is the story going to air or being published?'**

Make sure you see or hear it as soon as it does. If it's good news, share it with your networks, offline and online. If it's negative, and you weren't expecting that, consider issuing a response or contacting the reporter to discuss the story. This is tricky territory. Blasting a reporter or editor will never work. Approach with a tone of expressing your thoughts while being open to listening and learning at the same time. Remember: great media relationships are great for your business.

After you've covered those questions, tell the journalist you'll get back to her promptly. Even if you just give yourself ten minutes to review what you've gleaned, that's immensely helpful.

Make sure, too, that you always let a journalist know your title, and give the correct spelling of your name. A great journo will check that with you anyway, but don't risk it. There's nothing worse than seeing your name spelt incorrectly in a newspaper article or on the TV screen.

I was emailed recently by someone who started the message with 'Hi Trivia'. The 'c' is next to the 'v' on the keyboard, but that's no excuse. I emailed the guy back and told him I'd like to think I'm more important than trivia. I can only imagine how much more incensed I would have felt if I'd seen that published in an article, or pop up on the TV screen.

As for titles, they're important. Make sure the reporter has yours as 'manager', rather than 'employee', if that's what fits. I've never met a manager who'd rather be referred to as an employee.

WISE TALK MEDIA TIP 22 – NEVER CALL BACK BY THE DEADLINE

Many media trainers will tell you that you must call back a journalist before his deadline.

They're right. And, that's poor advice.

If a reporter rings you at 9.30am, tells you his deadline is 4pm, and you get back to him with the information he needs at 3.15pm … you're in trouble.

By then, he's most likely put together the bulk of his story, so he's slotting you in at the last minute to make sure you're represented. What that really means is that you've let go of the opportunity you were given to help shape the story. You've done nothing to better his understanding of your perspective or issues, and you also haven't had a chance to suggest other sources for the story who could complement what you have to say.

The bottom line is that what you say will have minimal impact. The entire exercise has been a waste of time—not just for you, but the reporter too. There's nothing that drives a journalist mad more than someone who never returns calls or comes back too late with information. It doesn't make a reporter think of you first when the next story arises, because you're hard work.

Instead, if the reporter rings you at 9.30am, tell him you'll get back to him within an hour (at the most). Then you'll be giving him what he needs from you long before he's even started writing his story. This gives you the power to help shape his perspective and influence the final story. It means he'll go to other interviewees and ask them to react to what you said, and then *those* people will be talking about what you said through your perspective—not theirs.

This was reinforced to me when I was recently interviewed for a newspaper article. A journalist called and asked me for some quotes. Using Wise Talk Media Tip 21, I asked her what the story was about, who she'd already spoken with, who else she was planning to speak with, and what she was hoping to achieve. I asked when her deadline was, and learned that the article would be a feature piece and she had the opportunity to spend a couple of days working on it—her deadline was two days away.

I wanted to be able to shape the story. I told her I'd like to email her my quotes, and would get them to her within two hours. The reason I wanted to email her the quotes (not that I told her this) was that I knew I'd craft my words better if I had the chance to write them out, rather than speak on the phone. She had no problem with that.

I emailed my quotes within two hours, as I said I would, and I sent eight paragraphs. I knew that was a lot more than the journalist needed, but I also knew that what I'd written was compelling and would be far better than the couple of sentences other interviewees would have given her over the phone.

The journalist said what I'd sent was great and thanked me, and guess what? The other person who was interviewed about the same topic, who'd answered a few quick questions over the phone, had three quotes in the story that went to press—about one-third of a column—while my words took up one-and-a-half columns.

That story was shaped—and dominated—by my perspective. I couldn't have asked for a better result.

The best advice I can give you is to return a reporter's call as quickly as possible. Aim to get back to him within an hour; fifteen minutes would be even better, especially during a crisis. Drop everything else you're doing? *Yes*. Absolutely.

WISE TALK MEDIA TIP 23 – START WITH WHY

A journalist needs to understand what your business or organisation does. You might get a broad question like, 'Can you tell me about your company?'

It's an invitation to ramble—although not designed that way—and nine times out of ten, a spokesperson will say something boring like, 'We're a software production company specialising in calendar systems and we have seventy-five employees in four different cities', or 'We're the leading supplier of eco-friendly products to health food stores in Australia'.

So what? Those statements are yawn-inducing.

It's your job to be enthusiastic and passionate when you're given an opportunity to speak about your organisation. Your best bet is to start with your 'Why' It provides meaning, and it's compelling.

Using the examples above, here's what the 'Why' could sound like:

'You know how these days everything is online, and it's getting harder to keep track of your diary because there are so many different calendars? Well, we produce an online calendar system that syncs all your diaries, it's quick and easy to use, and it's been such a success that we now have offices in four cities,' and, 'Well, more and more people are conscious of protecting the environment these days but they haven't been happy with the higher price of eco-friendly products and have questioned how well they work. We've figured out how to create a range of green products that are high quality and affordable.'

Notice the difference? Both statements are far more interesting than the first couple, and they naturally evoke further questions. That's a very good thing.

It's similar to an 'elevator pitch.' More than ever, your business needs to stand out ... but so do you. Where once brands belonged to cars and what you grabbed off the supermarket shelf, these days every single one of us has a brand.

When you're being interviewed by the media, you're being given the largest audience you'll likely ever have. Think about that for a moment. The largest audience!

Use the opportunity wisely. Start with 'Why'.

WISE TALK MEDIA TIP 24 — QUIT THE PERSONAL ATTACKS

As Australia's dozen new senators took their seats on the red benches at Parliament House for the first time, amidst advice to learn about their new surroundings and not allow themselves to be bullied, there was one senator who immediately blasted her way into the headlines.

During an interview on Radio National, Jacqui Lambie, a former army corporal, said the Prime Minister was a 'psychopath.' She also said he was a 'bare-faced and uncaring liar.'

After more personal attacks on the PM, Lambie suggested he take a bucket of cement and toughen up.

And now, everyone who reads or watches the news knows who Jacqui Lambie is. She's made her presence known in no uncertain terms, and she's done it fast.

Derogatory comments and personal attacks have become so commonplace in politics that we expect them. But do we respect the people who fuel such negativity? Do we trust them? Are we inspired to follow them? I'd suggest not.

Leave the politicians to play their game.

Go back to your Wise Talk Brand and remind yourself what you're all about. Don't perpetuate the negativity. Cut out any nasty talk.

Own your opportunity to inspire and lead during a media interview, no matter how hot your seat gets.

WISE TALK MEDIA TIP 25 –
WHEN TO SAY 'NO THANKS' TO AN INTERVIEW

Mostly, you want to say 'yes' to doing a media interview. It's a great way to build awareness of your business and, ideally, communicate your message to your target audience.

It gives you the chance to start building a relationship with a journalist. Get it right—by providing the information they need, being easy to work with, and great talent—and you'll likely get another call in the future.

But there are times when saying 'no' could be a wise choice. I say *could* because traditionally, there are certain situations where the rule has been not to make a comment. I'm going to tip some of those upside down for you.

Here they are:

Traditional advice:
A crisis has happened and employees haven't been notified, so it's best not to talk to the media.

My advice:
A reporter will run the story anyway. It's better to give your input, to ensure your provide the correct context. Also, using the media to share information could be wise if you can't logistically inform your employees directly before the story is published or goes to air.

Context is key here. For example, you wouldn't announce to

the media before telling your employees that you're closing down your operations and making 100 staff redundant. But if you announce a brand new product to the media before notifying employees, that could be strategically sound. You wouldn't want to run the risk of confidential information potentially being leaked to a competitor.

Traditional advice:

Lawyers have advised against communicating.

My advice:

Sometimes your silence will do you more harm than good. Even if you can't give specifics about an issue, it's essential to keep the conversation going. It can be as simple as a general comment like this: 'I can't give you specific information because it's a court matter, but there are always two sides to the story and we're confident that our side will come out when the time's right.'

I'm not a lawyer. I do recommend consulting with yours in this sort of situation. I also warn that lawyers have little concern for clear and genuine communication. As a communications professional, I suggest that speaking makes excellent sense, as long as you do it in a way that's aligned with how you want to be perceived.

Traditional advice:

You'll breach client, patient, or employee privacy if you talk to the media.

My advice:

It's never okay to do that. But you can make a generic comment. We don't trust people who keep walking and say, 'no comment' when there's a TV camera in their face.

That takes us to the next tip ...

CHAPTER 8:

WISE TALK MEDIA TIPS 26-30

WISE TALK MEDIA TIP 26 – WHAT NOT TO SAY

Journalists and their distrust aside, I want to ask you: When you see someone on TV say, 'no comment', what do you think about that person?

Do you think that person's guilty, being difficult, or simply has no interest in playing the media game?

Journalists think that person's trying to hide something, and they'll usually keep asking questions that become increasingly aggressive until the 'interviewee', who's refusing to be interviewed, walks into a coffee shop, gets in a car and drives away, or worse, punches a cameraman.

Whenever I was issued with a 'no comment', mostly when I was working for a TV current affairs program, it always made me more fiery, and didn't do any favours for the person refusing to speak to me. The words 'he wasn't available to comment' in the story that night smacked of a combination of having both something to hide and a feeling of smug superiority. That's the public perception.

Don't ever say, 'no comment'. Simply provide a generic answer, or explain why you can't answer the question. Be respectful and kind.

Here are more statements and questions to avoid:

1. **'Are you going to misquote me?'** Do I even need to explain why this is a dumb question? Questioning a journalist's professionalism will make her cross. She

won't put you in her little book of great talent. She'll avoid you for future opportunities.

2. **'Are you even going to use what I say?'** It's true that reporters ask lots of questions and use a small part of what you say. They're doing their job to get the information they need and the best quote from you. Get it right up front and they'll ask fewer questions, and you'll ensure that you get what you want in the story. Don't give a reporter a hard time.

3. **'That's a dumb question.'** This is on par with condescending looks that suggest what you're thinking without saying it. Some of the questions a journalist asks may well be dumb, according to you. Remember: you're the expert. You know more than the journo. It's your job to ensure that he understands the topic and has everything he needs. When you say a question is dumb, you're insulting the journalist. What does that achieve, other than to make you feel better? If you think a question is irrelevant, take the opportunity to explain the topic in more detail. With better understanding, the journalist might ask better questions.

4. **'I want to see the article before it's published.'** A reporter will not give you a copy of the article before it's published. When you ask to see it, you'll come across as paranoid and questioning the reporter's ability to do her job properly. When I was working in corporate communications writing articles for a client magazine, and didn't have a daily deadline, I did say 'yes' to one

request from a woman who wanted to see an article before it was published. I told her that I was happy to email her the article on the condition that she simply let me know if I'd made any factual errors. She sent the article back to me with all sorts of changes that were minor and mostly stylistic, according to how she thought the article should be written. My hackles were raised, to say the least. Checking a copy of an article before it's published, or a script before it goes to air, is the job of an editor. It's not yours.

WISE TALK MEDIA TIP 27 – KNOW WHERE TO LOOK

Eye contact is important. I know you know that. We respect and trust people who look us in the eye and maintain good eye contact.

When it comes to TV interviews, getting it right becomes complicated.

If you look in the wrong place, you can come across as nervous, unassured, evasive, or defensive. Not good news.

You also run the risk of being perceived as condescending or inadequate, depending on how the camera is positioned. If a camera is positioned in a way that it points up to your face, you'll look condescending. If it's positioned above you making you look up to it, you'll be perceived as inferior.

As I said, it gets complicated with TV, and what's most important to convey is that you're talking at the audience's level, not down to them or up to them. They need to feel equal for you to connect.

For a recorded TV interview, mostly likely in your office but possibly on the street outside your building or at another outside location, always look at the reporter who's asking you the questions. That means you're looking slightly off camera, as the reporter will usually stand next to the cameraman. I always suggest trying to imagine the camera isn't there. Just ignore it. I also recognise that's easier said than done!

For a live straight-to-camera interview, when the journalist or presenter is in the studio and you're elsewhere, you'll have an earpiece so you can hear the producer tell you when it's time for you to talk, or else you'll be listening for questions. For this sort of interview you need to look straight down the barrel of the camera lens.

This is tough if you're not used to it. For the entire interview you won't know exactly what's being shown because you can't see yourself, so you need to focus on maintaining eye contact with the camera the whole time. Looking around or looking away will make you look disinterested or uncomfortable at best—or evasive at worst.

The other part that's difficult is remembering your audience. You need to make a connection with viewers—to have a relationship with them—even though you can't see them.

It's a real skill to be able to do this. Some people think of a person they know and like, and imagine having a conversation with that person, in the tone they usually would.

Often, there's not much time to prepare for these sorts of interviews. If you do have time, get a video camera—even your smart phone will do—and practice speaking to it. Another option is to mark a spot on a wall and practice talking to it. Listen to how you sound. If you're not speaking in a way that sounds like you normally do, have another go. Aim to be natural.

A 'Sim-Sat' is the most difficult situation you're likely to find yourself in when it comes not only to where to look, but to speak naturally.

A sim-sat is a simulated satellite. You're interviewed on camera by a reporter who's in a different location. Via an ear bug, the reporter will ask you questions, and then the interview recording is fed out via satellite technology to be later aired on TV.

You might be required to look down the barrel of the camera lens for this, although often, producers prefer you to look to one side of the camera. If there's someone available to sit down for you to look at, in the right spot, it's easier to answer your questions because you're looking at a real person. It gets difficult though if there's no-one available, and you need to keep the correct eye line for the camera. That means you might need to look at a painting, or a spot marked on the wall, and "talk to it."

Sometimes a cameraman will use gaffer tape to mark an 'X' on a blank wall. Seriously. The cross will be there to ensure you keep the correct eye line with your interviewer—who you can't see. You need to stare at the wall, and imagine that person is sitting there and you can see a real face ... even though it doesn't exist. As I said, it's difficult. If you know you're taking part in a sim-sat, it's important to practice first. Place a cross— or even a piece of paper with a smiley face on it—on a wall and practice answering questions. It will feel strange, but it will make the experience less daunting when there's a real TV camera there.

Don't worry too much about in-studio interviews or panel discussions. Simply look directly at whoever's asking you the questions or doing the talking. The only tricky part in these situations is that there are other people in the studio who might distract you. There's a floor manager who might be walking around, and cameramen moving their cameras. Stay focused on what's happening on set, and you'll be fine.

WISE TALK MEDIA TIP 28 – CREATE MEMORABLE GRABS

A 'grab' is a term TV and radio journalists use. In the US they call it a 'sound bite'. It's the part of an interview the journo chooses to use in her story because it's catchy and attention grabbing.

Once you have your keywords and messages sorted on your Wise Talk Tree, it'll make it much easier to come up with aligned catchy quotes and grabs that reporters will want to use.

There are a range of styles of quotes and grabs:

1. **Emotional:** 'I'm appalled by the cruelty I've witnessed today, the worst it's been in twenty years of living in this city.'
2. **Three-punch:** 'We've been helping families who are struggling to pay their bills, and need rent assistance and food hampers to make ends meet.'
3. **Power:** 'We will not back down.'
4. **Superlatives:** 'Ballantyne Strong are the best digital stocks to invest in.'
5. **Rhetorical:** 'How many more people need to lose their jobs before the Government takes action?'
6. **Latest trends or pop culture:** 'If the weather continues like this, all we'll get is Five Seconds of Summer.'
7. **Cliches:** 'Time will tell, but not before we run out of it to get this project up and running.'
8. **Metaphors & Analogies:** 'They say life is like a box

of chocolates, and what we've been offered here is a classic example of that.'

9. **Contrasts:** 'The weather's hot, but it's going to take a cool customer to cope with these queues.'

* With thanks to Brad Phillips for help with this list

Politicians use these all the time, some more successfully than others. Independent Senator Nick Xenophon stands out for his ability to create great quotes and deliver them in a way that shows he's not just a politician, but a real human being with a sense of humour. He's renowned for his political stunts.

To protest against the Federal Government's decision to exclude Australian ship building firms from a one-billion dollar naval supply ship tender process, putting thousands of jobs at risk, Senator Xenophon teamed up with internationally renowned Elvis impersonator and performer, Mark Anthony. 'Elvis', all dressed up and toting his guitar, sang outside a city hotel in which the Defence Minister, David Johnston, was delivering a speech to business leaders.

Senator Xenophon said the Government's decision "leaves many 'suspicious' minds among Australia's defence industry," and the message from 'Elvis' is that we need "a little less conversation and a lot more action" on the part of the Government.

Corny perhaps, but Senator Xenophon is a favourite among the media, and the public. He's admired for his firm values and ability to connect with his audiences. He sees the political game for what it is, and continues to inject fresh and dynamic energy, and speaks like the rest of us.

Senator Xenophon has real conversations when the camera's turned off, usually including a few laughs. He's also a perfectionist, and known for stumbling with some of his answers to interview questions. In a recorded interview situation, he might answer the same question five or six times until he gets it right. It's testament to the relationships he's built with the media that no-one has ever taken advantage of the opportunity to undermine his credibility.

Remember, the media want you to be great talent. They want you to come up with a punchy quote. They want to use it in their story. Take a leaf out of Senator Xenophon's book.

First and foremost, always be yourself. If jokes aren't your cup of tea, leave them alone. So, too, clichés and pop culture. Choose a couple of styles of quotes and grabs that suit you and stick with them.

WISE TALK MEDIA TIP 29 – USE STRONG LANGUAGE

When Prime Minister Tony Abbott's election promise to ditch the carbon tax became a reality, he told Australians that it would boost confidence, with household savings including a drop in gas and electricity prices.

Mr Abbott said, "I certainly think it's good for confidence." He also said, "We're fulfilling our election promises and believe that's what Australians want."

Thinking it's good for confidence certainly doesn't instill confidence. Believing election promises are being fulfilled is akin to hoping that Father Christmas and the Easter Bunny are the real deal.

We don't want leaders who say they 'think' and 'believe' when they're standing up in front of us and expecting us to follow them. They sound tentative.

We need leaders who can *own it*.

What Mr Abbott should have said was, "It's good for confidence," and "We're fulfilling our election promises."

There's no place for any of these weak words and language from the mouths of leaders:

- 'I think'
- 'I guess'
- 'I hope'
- 'We might'

- 'We believe'
- 'It seems'
- 'We're trying'
- 'We may'

Instead, use these words:

- 'I know'
- 'Here's what we know'
- 'This will'
- 'It's clear that'
- 'We are doing'
- 'The evidence tell us'
- 'It will'

Say these out loud and notice the difference. It's palpable.

Language is powerful. Words matter. Be bold and declare what you're doing. Not only will you inspire trust, you'll also be so much more interesting.

WISE TALK MEDIA TIP 30 – LIFT YOUR ENERGY

When are you at your most energetic? When and where are you your most animated and engaged? And what are you talking about at the time?

It's important to know.

Your energy is one of your greatest allies in a broadcast interview. Most people aren't aware of their energy, nor how to consciously shift it to meet the situation.

While it's essential to be authentic and natural, speaking with the same energy level as you would in an ordinary conversation won't cut it on TV or radio.

In my early days of being a voice artist, my producer would keep telling me to stop sounding like a newsreader—even though I was one—and lift my energy. He'd tell me to put more into it, and made me read paragraphs again and again when he wasn't happy. It drove me mad. I understood what he was saying, though. How my voice over sounded to me, in my headphones, didn't sound the same once it had been recorded and played back.

When I first started working in TV, it was six weeks before I was allowed to be seen in a news story doing what's called a 'stand up', or 'piece to camera'. My cameraman would film me, and once we arrived back at the station the chief-of-staff would come into the editing suite and look at the tape and give me feedback. It was an excruciating process, as he told me what I was doing wrong and, worse, that I wasn't ready yet.

I'd always thought I'd done a pretty good job, but I could see that how I *felt* when I presented the piece to camera wasn't translating to the screen.

Somehow, microphones and TV screens 'flatten' what's being said. I learnt that I needed to over-compensate with extra energy. I also learnt that the easiest way to do that was by speaking louder.

It only takes an increase in volume of about ten to fifteen percent. There's no need to yell, nor fake it. There's no need to put on a performance—and there's definitely no need to be over the top.

You just need to be the most energised version of yourself.

No-one wants to listen to—nor takes much notice of—someone who sounds flat.

CHAPTER 9:

WISE TALK MEDIA TIPS 31-35

WISE TALK MEDIA TIP 31 – DITCH THE UMMS AND AHHS

Most of us can't stand silence. It makes us uncomfortable. And when we're uncomfortable about doing an interview, for example, the last thing we want is to feel more uncomfortable. So we talk. And we keep talking. And when a reporter's listening intently to what we're saying and uses silence to encourage us to keep going, what do so many of us do? We ramble. And we fill. We 'umm' and 'ahh' and say 'you know', and 'basically', and maybe even 'you know, like' or 'you know what I'm saying'?

It's a habit. Most of us do it. In a broadcast interview, it's distracting and undermining. When people are watching you and counting how many times you say 'you know', they're not listening to your message.

Pauses are your best friend if you use too many 'verbal fillers' to patch up the silence.

When you're asked a question, instead of answering straight away, take a moment to think about what you want to say before you say it. This is totally acceptable.

If you want to rid yourself of 'umms' and 'ahhs' and any other verbal fillers forever—which I highly recommend—try this exercise imparted to me by a veteran radio newsreader. When I was at university, I had private voice lessons with him, and he taught me to focus on speaking about a particular topic for thirty seconds. I was allowed to pause between sentences but couldn't use any filler words.

The trick was to come up with all sorts of random topics and speak about them.

He'd leave me in his studio, I'd switch on the microphone to talk, and my teacher would be in his office pressing 'record' on his old reel-to-reel tape machine. He'd play it back to me so we could listen out for any verbal fillers.

It takes time and patience, and it works. It's good practice to record yourself doing this and listening back to it to ensure no filler words turned up. This will help you break the habit.

Ultimately, you'll be far more engaging when you speak, which will help ensure your message is heard—and that's the whole point. You want your audiences to listen.

There are a few rules to remember when a crisis strikes:

1. **There'll be pain.** In the short-term, you and your organisation will likely suffer, but the negative impact doesn't need to be long-term. If you handle the crisis exceptionally well, the experience may well enhance your organisation's reputation. That means more loyalty from stakeholders, and it's good news for your bottom line. Know that those who show visionary leadership in a crisis have enormous power to inspire trust.

2. **Speak, and do it quick smart.** Share information as soon as you have it. Do your utmost to keep updating people. Even if you don't have much to say, it's enough to acknowledge that something serious has happened, and you're investigating, and as soon as you know more

you'll tell us. When you communicate immediately, it's likely you'll become the go-to source for information during the crisis. That gives you the opportunity to shape and influence the stories going to air and being published. It also builds your relationships with the media. Remember, too, that if you don't talk, someone else will. There'll be all sorts of people speculating about what's happened, and that just might fuel even more negative coverage.

3. **Make your responses about the victims.** Do I need to remind you that your audiences are filled with human beings? They care about other human beings, even complete strangers. Focus your communications on human safety and victims' needs. It's the most important factor, especially in the early hours of a crisis. Your audiences need to know that you care. We need to know that you're putting safety first. We need to know that, first and foremost, you're a human being. Then we might even feel empathy for you, too, and respect, and trust. The last thing we want is empty words. We don't want to be told that deaths are 'of serious concern', for example. Speak from your heart.

Remember, too, that this is more important than the facts. Yes, you need to share them, but the best response you can give addresses your audience's most pressing concerns. They're feeling pain and are shocked by tragedy. As horrific as such events are, they create connection and unite people in the fragile experience of life, death, and being human.

When the Malaysian Airlines flight was shot down by a surface-to-air missile over eastern Ukraine, killing 298 people—including 27 Australians—the Airline's chief executive spoke empathically about the priority of putting the victims first and contacting their families. Prime Minister Tony Abbott addressed Parliament saying it was a grim day for our country and a grim day for our world. 'Our hearts go out to the families of all the dead', he said. 'Our thoughts and prayers especially are with the families of the Australian dead. We can't restore them to life, but we can and will do everything to support them in this sad and bitter time because that is the Australian way'.

I'm sure Mr Abbott meant that everything would be done to support the victims' families, not the victims themselves. Regardless, the way he spoke didn't match his words. He might as well have been speaking about the latest budget figures.

The people killed when that plane was shot down were mothers, fathers, brothers and sisters, grandparents, children and friends. They were senselessly murdered by terrorists. It was a horrific crime that tore at the hearts of strangers around the world.

If ever there's a time to speak with heart, it's in a crisis situation like that. It isn't difficult. It just requires being human and aligned with what you're saying. There's no excuse for you, as a leader, not to connect with your words. When you don't, you alienate your audiences.

4. **Don't bury the bad parts.** Be upfront. Tell it as it is. Reveal the negative parts on your own terms rather than having someone else do it for you and hearing the news spread without your input. Hiding the bad parts can make the crisis worse. It also creates mistrust.

WISE TALK MEDIA TIP 33 – STAY CALM UNDER PRESSURE

You've nailed your messages. You've role-played and practiced interview scenarios. You've done all you can to prepare.

Then the TV crew shows up, and as the cameraman is setting up the camera on the tripod, plugging in and positioning the lights, and handing you the lapel microphone, and the journalist is chatting to you before the interview begins, you feel your heart start to race and your armpits getting sweaty.

Nervousness is normal. I want to go one step further and say that you need it. The sensations and intensity you feel in your body are preparing you to be 'on' and perform at your best. Instead of willing them to go away, your best bet is to welcome and embrace them. You need them.

Many people I work with tell me they want to 'get rid of' the intensity because it's uncomfortable. It's typical for most of us to want to avoid what doesn't feel good. The truth is, when you start to fight the sensations, they heighten. They create greater tension and more discomfort. When you welcome them, by accepting they're there to help you, it's possible to learn how to work with them for the greatest results.

You might have heard about the phenomenon of butterflies in your tummy, and learning how to get them to work together information. It's like that.

Here's how:

1. **Breathe.** There are great breathing exercises you can

do to slow down your heart rate, and calm and focus your mind. Try them before the media arrive. Even just five minutes will make a difference. Also focus on your Wise Talk Brand to help you get in the zone. This is essential. Aligning with it will help you enormously to ensure you speak in the way you want to be perceived. In one of my training sessions, a client told me she has a black belt in martial arts. To help her get in the zone, she 'puts on her black belt.' It works a treat.

2. **Stay in your body.** What I mean by this is that lots of people 'check out' when they find themselves in an uncomfortable situation. It's almost as if they've stepped outside their body and are watching it from the corner of the room. This is a sure fire way to increase anxiety, stumble, get your message mixed up, and forget what you wanted to say. You need to be present. You need to be in your body. The quickest and easiest way to do this is to breathe, and focus on your feet. The moment you take your attention to your feet, you'll be in your body and grounded. Plant your feet on the floor, rather than crossing your legs. Be aware of them on the floor. You might even want to imagine that your feet are super-glued to the floor, to help you stay grounded. If you notice yourself losing focus, concentrate on your feet for a moment to come back in to your body. Noticing the heaviness of your body on the chair can also help you to be present and grounded. I've seen these simple steps make a huge difference for many of my clients. Try them.

3. **Own the interview.** Remind yourself that the interview is happening on your terms. Take control. Use pauses to give yourself space to prepare your answers. Don't buy into toxic, negative questions. Wisely use questions as the gifts and opportunity they are to spread your message to your audience.

WISE TALK MEDIA TIP 34 – TAKE CHARGE IN MEDIA CONFERENCES

News, press, and media conferences are one and the same, and put you in a room filled with reporters competing to ask you the most difficult questions. Competition is key here. Each reporter wants to ask his questions, and there's limited time. It often takes interrupting other reporters and pushing in to be heard.

For you, there will likely be moments when you need to decide whose question you'll answer, as the reporters talk over top of one another.

Media conferences are tough. They require not only all the usual skills to take charge and be in control, but the ability to manage competition for your attention.

Media conferences are great for high interest stories as, with several media outlets in the same room, they can save you having to do several interviews about the same topic. In a crisis situation, holding a media conference sends a strong message that you're in control, and willing to talk about what's happened.

The best performers in a media conference, especially during a crisis:

1. **Ensure they're organised** before the media arrive, and walk into the room to speak once the media have set up their equipment. It shows they mean business and don't have time to waste.

2. **State their name** and title at the beginning of the media conference to ensure accuracy.

3. **Use simple messages** and speak them often, to set the record straight, dismiss errors, reduce speculation and misinformation, as well as to combat inaccurate reporting.

4. **Have a set time limit** and don't go beyond it. They decide how many questions they'll answer—and stick with that. They might say at the beginning of the media conference that they'll take six questions. This is a great way to make sure they're not perceived as running away when the going gets tough. Some don't do that, but simply announce that they'll take one more question, answer it, and then leave. If reporters keep asking them questions, they stick with their decision and walk out. Even if they are trying to avoid tough questions, but handle the situation with confidence and clarity, they'll likely get away with it.

5. **Keep eye contact** with the reporter asking the question. As there are likely several TV cameras there, as well as radio and newspaper journalists, they look straight at the questioner rather than try to ensure they're looking the right way for the cameras. They know that's the concern of cameramen, and not their problem.

6. **Take charge** by speaking in a way that's measured and deliberate. It gives the impression that they're con-

fident and competent to manage the situation. They stay calm and cool—but not cold.

7. **Keep their answers short**, on message and to the point. That ensures that there's a limit to the number of quotes reporters can use, enabling the interviewee to shape journalists' stories.

8. **Don't buy into reporters' games**. If they're talking over the top of one another, the interviewee chooses which question he wants to answer. If he can't hear the question clearly, he asks for it to be repeated. He works the room to suit his needs, and isn't swayed by negative questions or one-upmanship among reporters.

WISE TALK MEDIA TIP 35 – TELL GREAT STORIES

There are stories only you can tell, and they're the most powerful tool you have to illustrate and reinforce your messages.

According to most of my clients, their stories aren't very interesting or compelling. They think they need to come up with a cancer cure or fix the drought to be deemed worthy of attention. They think they need a 'big' story.

Many years ago, I remember interviewing a holistic vet who'd been working miracles for his canine patients. He had letters and cards of appreciation from pet owners who were more than willing to talk about how he'd turned around the health of their dogs. One woman said her aging dog had been on death's door, hardly able to walk, and could now race around the backyard like a puppy.

When I interviewed the vet, he tried to explain how some of his practices were different from those of regular vets. He was very matter of fact when he spoke, and uninspiring. To encourage more energy in his answers, I asked him to talk about some of his success stories. As he shared them, his speaking became livelier and richer. He talked about successfully treating a cat with cancer, which now had a new lease on life and was expected to live many more years. He reflected on the troubles an arthritic dog had, which could now walk daily around the block without any problem. His stories were interesting and captivating, easy to relate to, and meaningful for anyone with a love of animals.

A compelling story can be as simple as talking about a positive customer experience with your company or the impact of your work on the community.

To energise and inspire others, choose stories that:

1. **Focus on overcoming a challenge to achieve success**, just like the example of the holistic vet.

2. **Centre on developing relationships that bring people together and bridge a gap.** An example is the Choir of Hard Knocks, consisting of homeless and disadvantaged people, which received an Aria award for best original soundtrack and was well-received and applauded in public performances.

3. **Illustrate innovation or solving a long-held problem.** One example is biometrics for refugees fleeing violence in Syria. They arrive in Turkey with no identification, a major barrier to knowing how much help is needed and who needs it most. With biometrics, refugees' fingerprints are scanned to create a photo ID. It's used to access camp services, get meals, see doctors, and even find family who might be scattered among different camps.

You can also use one of the above three points if you're struggling to come up with relevant stories.

Think of a story to illustrate the most important parts of your message. For example, one client told me that a program her service ran helped decrease the youth suicide rate in her region.

That's great news, but it didn't make anywhere near as much impact until she shared a story about a particular teenager who was at high risk and then turned his life around with the help of the program. She talked about the problems he'd arrived with at the beginning of the program, and the specific changes he made in his life, including signing up to study at TAFE college. That made the message 'land', and memorable.

In all organisations there are great stories that, given the light of day, would support their message and help them connect with their audiences. When I'm working with a client, I'm often excited to hear a story that's considered ordinary and just part of the routine in an organisation—and not recognised for its inherent gold.

In every opportunity you get to share your message with an audience via the media, make sure you include stories. Each and every time. Then we'll connect with you, and remember you.

CONCLUSION

'I think it's so important to realise that we're here for others, we're here for the world, we're here for community. When you serve the world, when you serve other people, when you serve the ones you love, that's when you actually become elevated. That's when people look up to you. That's something we've lost sight of with all our leadership talk, and with all our "seven steps to being the pointiest, smartest, savviest, leader".

Dr Rachel Kohn, ABC Radio broadcaster

When this book was in the planning stages, I picked up a magazine I'd never heard of before while sitting in the waiting room for my monthly indulgence—a massage. I was early, and had time to read an interview with Rachel Kohn, presenter of the ABC Radio National program 'The Spirit of Things'. I jotted down the quote above and it stuck with me for days, then weeks.

When I sit down to write, I never really know what I'm going to say. I knew I wanted to write a book to serve leaders who find themselves in the media spotlight. I knew I had a depth of knowledge that only comes from getting one's hands dirty in the daily grind of delivering thousands and thousands of news and current affairs stories over many years. I knew I wanted to contribute to readjusting the imbalance of negativity we're constantly fed via the media. I also wanted to help empower leaders who, under the pressures and demands of difficult situations, encounter fear and frustration—and subsequently often don't handle the media nor communicate in a way that does justice to their leadership.

Dealing with the media and undertaking interviews in a way that allows you to influence—even control—the outcome of a story is entirely possible. It requires insider knowledge and enormous skill, as you've seen and learnt in the Wise Talk Media Tips I've shared with you.

I've interviewed thousands of leaders. I've trained, coached and presented to hundreds more. What I know is that when you take charge and place connection with your audiences *first*, your reputation will grow and you'll come out on top in even the most frightful of circumstances—even when you don't get all the techniques right.

For the first time since being sworn in as Prime Minister, Tony Abbott struck a positive chord with the majority of Australians for the way he handled the shooting down of the Malaysian Airlines plane over the Ukraine. Mr Abbott was the first world leader to stand up to Russian President Vladimir Putin and express his 'dissatisfaction' of the handling of the incident. He took swift action, leading the world—yes, the world—to do the right thing.

He was bold. He took a stand. Some have said he tapped into the horror, anger, and grief of our nation. However you choose to look at it, as the days wore on after the plane came down, and the push became tougher for access to the crash site, Mr Abbott did connect with us all. He showed strength and resolve to retrieve the bodies, investigate the site, and punish the guilty. He was compassionate. He spoke the words most Australians were thinking and saying over morning coffee with the newspaper, and in front of TV screens at night. He also showed a softer side—so rarely evident—and a depth of feeling. You might even dare to call that vulnerability, if you choose to define it as emotional exposure.

It's common that leaders' popularity rises after a crisis. Former Queensland Premier, Anna Bligh, will long be remembered for how she handled the 2010-2011 floods.

Thirty-five people were killed. Two-hundred thousand were affected in at least seventy towns. Three-quarters of council areas in Queensland were declared disaster zones.

With messy hair, little to no make-up, and looking as though she'd been up all night working, Anna Bligh spoke wholeheartedly at media conferences. There were tears, at times, as she spoke about the devastation and hardship for local communities. She spoke proudly of what it means to be a Queenslander—'the people they breed tough, north of the border'. As if channelling what most Australians were thinking, she spoke of weeping for what had been lost, of grief for family and friends, and confronting the challenges that lay ahead.

She spoke of the strengths of Queenslanders being knocked down and getting up again.

Anna Bligh's emotional appeal hit social media within moments, and her name was a trending topic across the country, spreading quickly to the world. She was applauded for speaking frankly and sincerely. She was called a 'truly awesome lady'. Many said she demonstrated the difference between leadership and merely being the leader of a political party.

The Queensland floods defined Anna Bligh's leadership. They turned around her political fortunes, putting her ahead of the Liberal party after many months of poor polling. That was heavily reported—as if it were the most important thing. It was a symbol though, and even a symptom, of her ability to unite her community and the nation by taking charge, doing what needed to be done, informing us all the way and, most powerfully of all, connecting with us—human to human, displaying genuine empathy combined with strength, determination, and fierce decision-making.

During war and natural disasters, horrific crimes and terrorist attacks, it's crude to suggest that leaders have fresh opportunities to show different sides of their character. It's unfortunate, too, that that's what it takes. There are frequent opportunities—daily, in fact—to connect with team members, clients, and customers as a wise leader, regardless of whether or not it's in the eye of the media. Much of what's been revealed in this book will help you become a more effective communicator—and leader—in all sorts of forums.

And when there are TV cameras pointing in your direction? Or the microphone's on and the red 'live on air' light is flashing? The foundations of how you respond needn't nor shouldn't be any different. Use every opportunity you're given to approach journalists' questions as gifts and turn them into diamonds.

Don't drop the *lead* in leadership. Remind yourself what matters most, then focus on the skills and techniques you've learnt here so you can nail media interviews. Develop your Wise Talk Brand. Choose *purposeful*, *personal* and *powerful*. Share the messages and stories you know are the most important to tell, influence and shape the outcome of what journalists say about you, and inspire and lead every time you speak.

Media interviews are your greatest chance to influence and serve the largest audience you'll ever have: the public.

We need you to rise to the occasion.

FINAL THOUGHTS...

Thank you for taking the time to read this book. Its contents have given you plenty that will help you prepare for the next time you're faced with dealing with the media. My hope is that you see the gifts in every opportunity to influence and shape the outcomes of media coverage, and connect with your largest audience – the public.

It is challenging. It takes skill and practice. And, it's worth your investment – and reputation and business outcomes – to get it right.

As I've said a few times in this book, journalists are human too. They usually respond well to people who make an effort to build relationships with them that are based on sincerity, generosity and integrity.

Reporters want to do a good job, and they want you to be great talent. It makes their stories better, and it gives you golden opportunities to spread your message – and shine.

I wish you the very best.

You're welcome to contact me directly with your feedback or questions at tricia@wisetalk.com.au.

THE WISE TALK OFFER

Are you ready to turn every media opportunity into a win for your business?

Would you love to achieve more media coverage?

Having read this book, you understand that dealing with the media – and achieving your desired outcomes – requires insider knowledge, learning new skills, and practicing them, under the guidance of a communications professional who has broad journalism experience.

As a special offer and 'thank you' for reading this book, Wise Talk is offering a free *Media Ready* audit, valued at $500. I, or one of my team members, will call your business and spend half an hour reviewing your current media strategies, processes and goals. You'll then be provided with a written report on areas to improve.

To take advantage of this free offer, please email:
audit@wisetalk.com.au
to arrange your appointment, or visit us at
www.wisetalk.com.au.

ABOUT THE AUTHOR

Tricia Karp, Founder & CEO, Wise Talk

Tricia's expertise is maximising outcomes for leaders communicating in high-pressure, high-stakes situations.

Often referred to as a "multimedia miracle worker," Tricia spent 20 years working in the media as an award-winning prime time TV and radio news presenter, news and current affairs journalist, news director and voice artist. She worked at Channel 7, commercial and ABC radio, and as a senior corporate communications adviser for a global company.

Tricia specialises in media, presentation skills and powerful presence corporate training and coaching. She's passionate about guiding leaders to ensure they inspire and communicate leadership, especially in situations that demand their greatest response.

An engaging professional speaker herself, Tricia is known as an inspiring communicator who easily connects with, and motivates, a wide variety of audiences.

Her first book, *Own It: Powerful Speaking for Powerful Women*, is a #1 Amazon bestseller.

www.ingramcontent.com/pod-product-compliance
Lightning Source LLC
Chambersburg PA
CBHW070754290326
41931CB00011BA/2013